Formal Cause in Marshall McLuhan's Thinking

An Aristotelian Perspective

By Laura Trujillo Liñán

INSTITUTE OF GENERAL SEMANTICS

Copyright © 2022 by Laura Trujillo Liñán

All rights reserved. No part of this publication may be reproduced or transmitted in any form or by any means, electronic or mechanical, including photocopying, recording, or by any information storage and retrieval system, without permission in writing from the publisher.

Published by the Institute of General Semantics
72-11 Austin Street, #233
Forest Hills, New York, 11375
www.generalsemantics.org

Interior Book Design by Scribe Freelance
www.scribefreelance.com

Published in the United States of America
ISBN: 978-1-970164-18-3 (Print)
978-1-970164-19-0 (eBook)

Cover illustration based on image title: *Marshall McLuhan in the early 1970's*, copyright © Library and Archives Canada. Reproduced with the permission of Library and Archives Canada.

Source: Library and Archives Canada/Horst Ehricht Fonds/PA-198674

Library of Congress Cataloging-in-Publication Data

Names: Trujillo Liñán, Laura, author.
Title: Formal cause in Marshall McLuhan's thinking : an Aristotelian perspective / Laura Trujillo Liñán.
Description: Forest Hills, New York : Institute of General Semantics, [2022] | Series: New non-Aristotelian library | Includes bibliographical references. | Summary: "The concept of formal cause was originally by the ancient Greek philosopher Aristotle, in his treatise on metaphysics, later elaborated upon by the medieval philosopher Thomas Aquinas, and more recently claimed by the modern media philosopher Marshall McLuhan. Introduced as one of four types of causality, alongside that of material cause, efficient cause, and final cause, McLuhan adopted formal causality in an effort to explain the effects of media and600 technology. This study reviews, compares, and contrasts Aristotle's and McLuhan's understanding of formal cause in relation to contemporary media theory, non-aristotelian systems, and the field of media ecology"-- Provided by publisher.
Identifiers: LCCN 2022031455 (print) | LCCN 2022031456 (ebook) | ISBN 9781970164183 (print) | ISBN 9781970164190 (ebook)
Subjects: LCSH: God. | McLuhan, Marshall, 1911-1980. | Aristotle. | Causation.
Classification: LCC BL473 .T78 2022 (print) | LCC BL473 (ebook) | DDC 122--dc23/eng/20220810
LC record available at https://lccn.loc.gov/2022031455
LC ebook record available at https://lccn.loc.gov/2022031456

BOOKS in the IGS Book Series
New Non-Aristotelian Library

Korzybski, Alfred (2010). *Selections from Science and Sanity*. (2nd Ed.). Edited by Lance Strate, with a Foreword by Bruce I. Kodish. Fort Worth, TX: Institute of General Semantics.

Strate, Lance (2011). *On the Binding Biases of Time and Other Essays on General Semantics and Media Ecology*. Fort Worth, TX: Institute of General Semantics.

Anton, Corey (2011). *Communication Uncovered: General Semantics and Media Ecology*. Fort Worth, TX: Institute of General Semantics.

Levinson, Martin H. (2012). *More Sensible Thinking*. New York, NY: Institute of General Semantics.

Anton, Corey & Strate, Lance (2012). *Korzybski and. . .* (Eds.) New York, NY: Institute of General Semantics.

Levinson, Martin H. (2014). *Continuing Education Teaching Guide to General Semantics*. New York, NY: Institute of General Semantics.

Berger, Eva & Berger, Isaac (2014). *The Communication Panacea: Pediatrics and General Semantics*. New York, NY: Institute of General Semantics.

Pace, Wayne R. (2017). *How to Avoid Making A Damn Fool of Yourself: An Introduction to General Semantics*. New York, NY: Institute of General Semantics.

Lahman, Mary P. (2018). *Awareness and Action: A Travel Companion*. New York, NY: Institute of General Semantics.

Levinson, Martin H. (2018). *Practical Fairy Tales For Everyday Living, Revised Second Edition*. New York, NY: Institute of General Semantics.

Levinson, Martin H. (2020). *Sensible Thinking for Turbulent Times: Revised Second Edition*. New York, NY: Institute of General Semantics.

Mayer, Christopher (2021). *How Do You Know?: A Guide to Clear Thinking About Wall Street, Investing, and Life*. New York, NY: Institute of General Semantics.

Levinson, Martin H. (2021). *Practical Fairy Tales For Everyday Living, Revised Second Edition*. New York, NY: Institute of General Semantics. (In Spanish)

Table of Contents

Acknowledgements... vii
Foreword ix
Introduction 13
Analysis of Aristotle's and Marshall McLuhan's Theories of Formal Cause... 19
    Formal Cause According to Aristotle 19
    Formal Cause According to Marshall McLuhan 27
    The Relationship Between Formal Cause and Media 31
"The Medium is the Message"................................... 45
Media's Qualities as the Individual's and Society's Formal Cause.... 65
    Speech as Formal Cause 67
        Words and Essence 67
        Words and Subject....................................... 73
        Orality and *Trivium* 76
        Language and Its Relation to the Development of Culture .. 81
        Speech and Its Relation to Mimesis......................84
    Written Language as the Foundation of Individuality 95
    Contemporary Media and Their Influence on Humans......... 106
Marshall McLuhan's Formal Cause Is, in Fact, Aristotle's Efficient Cause... 116
    Formal Cause as Intrinsic v. Efficient Cause as Extrinsic to the Being... 116
Conclusions 123
Bibliography 127
About the Author 131

Acknowledgements

This effort would not have been possible without the invaluable support of my husband Ricardo, who has dedicated his life to promoting my professional and personal advancement. I also want to thank my children: Ricardo, Laura, Roberto and María José because without their support, their encouragement, their patience, and their affection, I would not have been able to achieve what I have done so far.

I especially want to thank Lance Strate for his support throughout this process, for the time spent making corrections, for seeking support from reviewers to get this work out, for his recommendations, and for having the openness to consider different perspective, and the patience to listen and to understand. I remember being invited by him to attend my first Institute of General Semantics symposium, and without that invitation, I would hardly have had the opportunity to join a community of intellectuals with a great sense of humanism, and humanity, and the openness to listen to people from other latitudes. Thanks also for your prologue, which manages to synthesize the essence of this work and unite ideas of great intellectuals in history such as Aristotle, Alfred Korzybski and Marshall McLuhan. This work has involved hours, days, months of attention, work, corrections and many emails, and I am grateful for all of this support.

I cannot fail to mention the person who brought me closer to media ecology for the first time, Thom Gencarelli, to whom I will always be grateful for allowing me to participate in the 2011 Media Ecology Association convention with my first international presentation at Manhattan College, despite having closed the Call of Papers on that occasion. There for the first time I met so many wonderful people who have helped and supported me throughout all these years. It is important to note that it was at one of the MEA meetings conferences that I was invited to attend to the Institute of General Semantics symposium.

Finally, I want to thank the Institute of General Semantics Board of Trustees for allowing me to be an active part of this organization and for accepting the publication of this text. I hope I can contribute something of value in return for how much you have already given me.

Foreword

Lance Strate
President, Institute of General Semantics

Every so often I am asked to explain why general semantics is referred to as *non-aristotelian*. Or I'm simply asked, *What do you have against Aristotle?* Or, *what did Alfred Korzybski have against Aristotle?* In other words, the designation *non-aristotelian* is sometimes interpreted as the equivalent of being *anti-aristotelian*. And nothing could be further from the case.

After all, Korzybski was schooled in the Catholic intellectual tradition, in fact was the product of Jesuit education, before going on to study engineering. That kind of classical education was based on the trivium, the curriculum of the medieval university (an institution that was the equivalent of our secondary school, their mission being to train boys for the priesthood or other forms of clerical service). The trivium itself had its roots in antiquity, in the study of rhetoric, grammar, and dialectic or logic, all of which were addressed by Aristotle. Of course, Aristotle was not the first to deal with these subjects, but he was the first great systematizer of the ancient world. And his treatises on rhetoric, poetics, and logic were later summarized and supplemented by other scholars, among them the Catholic philosopher and theologian, Thomas Aquinas. It is through this tradition that Korzybski was first exposed to Aristotelian thought. It should come as no surprise, then, that Margaret Gorman was able to identify significant parallels between his general semantics and Thomism, the philosophy of Thomas Aquinas in her doctoral dissertation and subsequent publication, *General Semantics and Contemporary Thomism*.

To allay any lingering doubts about Korzybski's view of Aristotle, you need not look any further than the dedication page of the magnum opus, *Science and Sanity*, where Aristotle is listed as the first of 55 names that appear (in alphabetical order, admittedly, but arguably that choice was made because it did allow Aristotle to be listed first). We can also note that Korzybski was specifically concerned with developing a *system*, and Aristotle essentially invented the idea of systems of thought or ideas. In this sense, Korzybski saw himself as following in Aristotle's footsteps, or standing on his shoulders, as it were. But this involved more than a neo-aristotelian turn, or return, but rather the development of altogether new systems. Specifically, *Science and*

Sanity was Korzybski's answer to Aristotle's *Organon*, which was devoted to the topic of deductive logic. Significantly, some three centuries earlier, Francis Bacon had the same goal in mind when he published his *Novum Organum*, the title a direct allusion to the *Organon*. The 17th century treatise established the foundation for modern scientific method, arguing for a new logic based on inductive reasoning and reductionism. That Bacon is not included on Korzybski's dedication page is perhaps reflective of a gap in his education, as he studied science, mathematics, and engineering, not the philosophy of science. It is interesting to note that Marshall McLuhan's posthumously published book, *The Laws of Media*, co-authored by Eric McLuhan, does reference Bacon directly, and alludes to the *Novum Organum* in the subtitle, *The New Science*.

The *Science and Sanity* dedication page does include Albert Einstein, as well as Hermann Minkowski, Niels Bohr, and Werner Heisenberg, among others, whose work in science and mathematics resulted in the paradigm shift from Newtonian to what became known as *non-Newtonian* physics (Isaac Newton is also included among the 55 names). Although later eclipsed by the term Einsteinian physics, at least in regard to astrophysics, non-Newtonian physics was complemented by new kinds of geometries necessary for dealing with the curvature of space, and later subatomic physics; this was referred to as *non-Euclidean geometry* (Euclid is also one of the 55). These early 20th century neologisms served as Korzybski's model, as he set about to develop a new system of thought to compliment these new notions about the nature of reality. It made perfect sense, then, for Korzybski to use the combining form of *non-* in naming his new system.

Moreover, in his reference to Aristotelian thought, Korzybski was not criticizing the entirety of Aristotle's philosophy, just as Einstein was not critiquing the entirety of Newton's work, which includes, for example, the development of calculus in mathematics. Rather, Korzybski was concerned very specifically with Aristotle's *Organon*, and subsequently how Aristotelian logic was taught by his followers down through the ages, from antiquity to the medieval period to the modern age (and how it served as the default, common sense mode of thought, at least in western cultures). Like Bacon, Korzybski found this approach to be inadequate, but not just for high-minded philosophical investigation or specialized scientific research, but in general, for everyone. For this reason, he pointed to the need for non-aristotelian systems to complement non-newtonian physics and non-euclidean geometry, but also to create a paradigm shift in education, and in the thinking of the general population. His solution was of his own invention, his non-aristotelian system of general semantics. It was designed as a system of thought that better reflected the new scientific understanding of reality as based on relativity rather than absolutes, probability rather than certainty, change rather than permanence.

While non-newtonian physics superseded Newton's physics, it did not eliminate the older science entirely, but positioned it as a special case within the larger understanding of relativity. Along the same lines, Korzybski did not invalidate Aristotle's logic, instead reducing it to a special case within a much more expansive system of general semantics. I would also argue that had Korzybski been operating in the late 20th century instead of the 1930s, he no doubt would have instead termed his system *post-aristotelian*, following the example of postmodernism, posthumanism, and the like. And indeed, this would have been a better map for the territory that he was exploring.

As for the relationship between non-aristotelian systems and general semantics, it is worth noting the subtitle of Korzybski's *Science and Sanity*, which reads, *An Introduction to Non-Aristotelian Systems and General Semantics*. It is no accident that the reference is to *systems* in the plural, as Korzybski acknowledged that general semantics was *a* non-aristotelian system, not *the* non-aristotelian system. In other words, he recognized the potential and the actuality of other such systems, for example Charles Sanders Peirce's semiotics, Alfred North Whitehead and Bertrand Russell's theory of logical types, and Charles Darwin's theory of natural selection, as well as Claude Shannon's information theory, Norbert Wiener's cybernetics, and Gregory Bateson's systems theory, along with later elaborations such as chaos and complexity theory, fractal mathematics, and the concepts of emergence and autopoiesis.

To all this we can also add media ecology as a non-aristotelian entry, with the caveat that it is not exactly a system, but certainly a set of ideas and an approach. In particular, the resonances with Marshall McLuhan are undeniable, despite the fact that their backgrounds were entirely disparate, McLuhan being immersed in the humanities as a literary scholar turned media maven, Korzybski being dedicated to bringing a scientific, mathematical, and engineering perspective to the masses. And yet both were public intellectuals in their own right, with a multitude of followers, and both following the Thomist philosophy of privileging sense perception above all else. McLuhan, in his doctoral dissertation, notably gives favorable mention to Korzybski as a fellow grammarian working against the dominant intellectual strain of the logicians, in favor of understanding the primary role of language. Korzybski's untimely demise in 1950 did not allow for him to become familiar with McLuhan's work, but within the general semantics community, including Korzybski's close associates, McLuhan was well received. It eventually fell to Neil Postman to link the two together under the heading of media ecology, which Postman referred to as *general semantics writ large*. More recently, other works, including books published in this New Non-Aristotelian Library series, have also dealt with the field of media ecology.

Laura Trujillo Liñán's study focuses on the concept of formal cause, which originates via Aristotle's *Metaphysics*, and which I would characterize, in contrast to his *Organon*, as a decidedly non-aristotelian Aristotle (human beings can be contradictory, as evidenced by Newton's writings on the occult). Here too we encounter Thomas Aquinas, as he further developed Aristotle's notions of causality, specifically the four causes designated formal, final, material, and efficient. And once again, modern science gets into the act, as reductionism eliminates all but one of them, efficient cause, the causality we associate with the mechanistic, cause-and-effect thinking associated with Newtonian physics. Whether conscious of it or not, in developing general semantics, Korzybski was seeking to go beyond efficient cause and the related notion of material cause; arguably, he was attempting to retrieve or reinvent the concepts of formal and final causality that better relate to cybernetics and systems, to biological and psychological processes, and to relativity and uncertainty. As an alternative to Newtonian physics, formal and final causality correspond to the science developed by Leonardo da Vinci, with its focus on complex processes and organic phenomena. McLuhan was quite explicit in referencing formal cause as the basis of his understanding of media and technology, and their effects, and this was further elaborated upon by his son and collaborator, Eric McLuhan, followed by other media ecology scholars.

As we continue to develop the philosophy and practice of non-aristotelian systems, we need to continue our explorations of the aristotelian systems that they build upon, to better understand what they have to offer us, and what their limitations may be. In his time, Aristotle recognized the need for new systems of thought and logic to meet the demands of his newly literate society, and the struggle to create and maintain new forms of civilization. A century ago, Korzybski realized the need for new systems of thought to meet the demands of a rapidly modernizing society characterized by myriad new forms of media and communication, and the struggle to make progress as a civilization. Several decades later, McLuhan articulated the need for new systems of thought to make sense of the speed and scope of technological change and the entirely new media environments that envelop us, and the struggle to maintain some kind of civilization. Today we surely realize the necessity of new modes of thought and the need for expanding and evolving individual and collective consciousness, and the struggle for the very survival of the human race. To this end, Laura Trujillo Liñán's philosophical investigation makes an important contribution.

Introduction

Over two millennia ago, philosophy arose as a system of thought developed by a group of thinkers in Ancient Greece who aimed to set aside subjectivity and understand the world objectively. It is reputed that in sixth century BC, Thales of Miletus was the first to express a philosophical argument that water was the origin, or *Arche*, of all that exists. From then on, more thinkers became interested in studying the physical, and later, metaphysical principles of the universe.

Most Western philosophical theories developed in this context, and chiefly among them was Aristotle from Stagira, a Greek city now heralded as his birthplace. Much has been said about Aristotle's philosophical contributions, although little is known about his private life. Expressly, he died at the age of 62 during the fall of 322 BC and is memorialized as one of the most prominent public intellectuals of his time, who captivated and inspired male youth of Greece in the challenging time. According to Jonathan Barnes, one of Aristotle's most prominent biographers, "no man before him had contributed so much to learning."[1] As a man born into a wealthy family, Aristotle was able to be well-dressed and hone excellent public speaking skills. However, because of this he was often accused of arrogance by his enemies. Outside of this, little else is known about him due to a lack of evidence and testimonies lost in time.

Based on his writings and approach, one might argue that Aristotle's primary objective was to promote the discovery of truth and catalyze a pursuit of knowledge. To achieve this, he asked for the help of various male intellectuals in efforts to further investigate their experience. In this sense, one can find Aristotelian works on practically any topic: animals, ethics, poetry, physics, metaphysics, logic, and more. Due to the vastness of this undertaking, he consulted many men to help him understand the world, and his legacy has impacted all of Western knowledge. Many of his definitions, concepts, and fields of knowledge, like logic, prevail to this day, nearly unchanged.

As such, some contextual errors in Aristotelian theory have been uncovered over the past two thousand years. Concepts and ideas that were then products of limited scientific and technological knowledge(s) can now be studied more

---

1 Barnes, Jonathan. *Aristotle: A very short Introduction*. New York: Oxford University Press, 2000 p. 1

precisely and/or from broader perspective(s).

For example, general semantics offers a non-Aristotelian vision of life and the world. In this sense, while Aristotle sought out Truth through dialectics and the universalization of knowledge, Korzybski opts for an alternative, non-Aristotelian view which, through induction and empiricism, intended to reach truth in a more multiplicitous way. In other words, Korzybski offered the language of sanity which he argued promoted effective communication and understanding of others. For him, general semantics encouraged humane behaviors in a world that disconnected us from ourselves in order to pay attention to the general. He proclaimed this mentality led us to forget the human being in pursuit of science. According to Korzybski's view, whole-sale acceptance of an Aristotelian persuasion has led scientists to hide individual's true being, which should not be forgotten. At the end of the day, those who generate knowledge and those for whom knowledge is generated are human beings. In Korzybski's words:

> "The non-Aristotelian system presented here has turned out to be a strictly empirical science, as predicted, with results which have greatly surpassed even my expectations. General semantics is not any 'philosophy, or 'psychology, or 'logic', in the ordinary sense. It is a new extensional discipline which explains and trains us how to use our nervous systems most efficiently (...) 'Philosophers', 'psychologists', logicians', mathematicians', etc., are somehow unable to comprehend that their work is the product of the working of *their own nervous systems.*"[2]

In order to understand Korzybski's thinking and, thus, gain a clearer idea of what General Semantics theory entails, and the importance of its claims, we must first become familiar with some of Aristotle's key concepts. To demonstrate, see the table below presented by Alfred Korzybski in *Science and Sanity,* denoting his concepts that I utilize throughout this manuscript:[3]

---

2   Korzybski, Alfred. *Science and Sanity*. New York: Institute of General Semantics, 1993 p. xxxviii-xl
3   Korzybski Alfred. *Science and Sanity*. New York: Institute of General Semantics, 1993, pp. lii-liii

Old Aristotelian Orientations (Circa 350 B.c.)	New General Semantic Non-Aristotelian Orientations (1941 A.c.)
Static, 'objective,' 'permanent,' 'substance,' 'solid matter,' etc. orientation	*Dynamic*, ever-changing, etc., electronic process orientation
'Properties' of 'substance,' attributes,' 'qualities' of 'matter,' etc.	Relative invariance of function, dynamic structure, etc.
Two-valued causality, and so consequent 'final causation'	Infinite-valued causality, where the 'final causation' hypothesis is not needed

An additional point of comparison:[4]

Abstraction, what is universal, essence	Abstraction, levels of knowledge according to the being

As the above table shows, there are very clear differences between both theories; however, they both have to do with very concrete time and space. In the case of Aristotle, we are dealing with a third-century BC author, while with Korzybski, we are referring to a man who lived within the past century. It would be somewhat unfair to attempt a comparison of such temporally distant and disparate theories, yet it is necessary in order to be able to adequately understand and analyze them. Additionally, I include a third author to help readers better understand the two former: Marshall McLuhan. I chose McLuhan for two main reasons. First, his articulations of causality, which were also of great importance to Aristotle being that he used this concept in claims to objective knowledge attainment. And, secondly, McLuhan's use of abstraction, that are also integrally linked to Korzybski's work because he claimed it was through this term that we know the world. For Korzybski, the process of abstraction is how we are able to theoretically capture an object for a moment, stop its movement, other changes, and dynamism, abstracting and enabling something to know it. In Marshall McLuhan's work, this process would be impossible without usage of media. Hence why he is known as a pioneer of the field of Media Ecology, an approach that asserts mediation has become part of our nature, which we employ to understand the world.

In this way, Marshall McLuhan's theory can serve as a basis to extend understanding of Aristotle and Korzybski. And, furthermore, Media Ecology is a means to explore these authors and the differences between them, or as Strate

---

4   This is my own contribution

asserts: "With this way of understanding media, we can say that we relate to our environments through a process of mediating, of interfacing, of abstracting.⁵"

By conducting a comparative analysis of Aristotle, Korzybski, and McLuhan, I convey a clearer idea of what unites and separates these authors to document how their theories gleam different understandings about the world, truth, and undivorceable human and societal connection.

> In doing so, we encounter three different disciplines that converge towards a shared goal: the human process of making-sense of life on earth. However, each author studied this from a different perspective. Philosophy attempted to provide an explanation for human behavior based on its ultimate causes and fundamental principles. While communication sought to convey clear and truth-based information, so that humans may properly develop in society.

The method I apply throughout this study is based on a comparison between two very important scholars. The first, the philosopher Aristotle, created a theory of four causes to explain reality, and thus, humanity. The next, communication scholar Marshall McLuhan, saw the medium as the message, explaining the influence of medias on society. At the heart of the comparison of both observations lies the concept of formal cause, as it is of essential significance when explaining both their writings. In Aristotelian philosophy, it provides humans' reason for being, as it is intrinsic to them. Whereas, McLuhan, saw the raison d'etre as extrinsically found in medias, as is further demonstrated in my analysis herein.

As such, throughout this manuscript, I first expound on the Aristotelian position regarding the four causes, as these consist of the foundation to subsequent understanding of Marshall McLuhan's "formal cause," as well as that of other scholars. In addition, this allow a clarification of the main meaning of formal cause, in order to suitably compare it to McLuhan's vision and detail some similarities and differences. Secondly, I demonstrate how McLuhan identifies the medium as formal cause and the significance of this. Moreover, I explain his definition of "medium" so as to operationalize his perspective, and thus, provide a precise comparison with Aristotelian philosophy. Thirdly, I illustrate ways medias behave as society's formal cause, while exploring the effects they have on different societies, thus, analyzing McLuhan's position from a historical perspective. Fourth, I focus on the comparison between Aristotle's formal cause and that of McLuhan, in order to analytically find

---

5   Strate Lance. "Korzybski, Luhmann, and McLuhan" in *Proceedings of the Media Ecology Association*, Vol. 11, 2010, p. 5

commonalities and differences between the two, and indicate any potential usefulness of Aristotelian formal cause in Marshall McLuhan's work. Therefore, as stated at the beginning of this essay, I illuminate a communication-based bridge between two eminently related sciences. Specifically, how their subjects of study coincide in diverse ways, uniting them despite each author's language usage distinctions. In other words, these linguistic differences drive them apart, orienting away possibilities of reconciliation between them.

Based on this link of "formal cause" and utilizing philosophical categories, we will be able to understand and analyze Marshall McLuhan's theory on the impact of media on humans and attain a better understanding of humans and society based on interdisciplinary dialogue.

This theme was thoroughly developed by Eric McLuhan in his book, *Media and Formal Cause*,[6] in his article, "Concerning Media Ecology" in *Explorations in Media Ecology*,[7] and was further explored in "Taking Up McLuhan's Cause: Perspectives on Media and Formal Causality."[8] The importance of this subject lies in comprehending society's function based on the use of media. In this sense, just as for Korzybski, the way we perceive our environment and ourselves leads us to act certain ways. According to Marshall McLuhan and Eric McLuhan, the way we perceive reality through different medias not only orient us into certain behaviors, but also influences how we are able to think:

> Formal cause is the causality of emergent properties, the causality that media ecologist often have in mind when we consider the impact of technological change on the individuals and societies, on communication, consciousness, and culture.[9]

In this sense, Eric McLuhan denotes the role and influence French philosophers, such as Étienne Gilson and Jacques Maritain, had on Marshall McLuhan's thinking regarding formal cause. In fact, he cited unpublished letters containing crucial resources for enhanced understanding of this theory:

> But while he knew (Marshall McLuhan) the route to understanding media new or old was to be traced in the actions of environments and not of their contents or uses, the matter of an appropriate causality still

---

6   McLuhan, M, McLuhan E. *Media and Formal Cause*. NeoPoiesis Press, Texas 2011
7   McLuhan, Eric. "Concerning Media Ecology." *Explorations in Media Ecology*, vol. 5, no. 3, 2006, pp. 185–198., https://doi.org/10.1386/eme.5.3.185_1.
8   Anton, Corey, et al. *Taking up McLuhan's Cause: Perspectives on Media and Formal Causality*. Intellect, 2017.
9   See: Lance Strate in McLuhan Marshall, McLuhan Eric. *Media and Formal Cause*. NeoPoiesis Press, LLC., Texas 2011, p. x

eludes him. In 1969, he wrote to Jacques Maritain:

> I am quite aware that nobody has attempted to understand metamorphosis and causality in social institutions through a minute inspection of the sensory and perceptual changes resulting from the new environments. Surely the history of philosophy can never be written without a complete awareness of these matters.[10]

Maritain responded by urging him to pay more attention to formal cause:

> I am overall in agreement with what you have written to me... This, in its way, plays an essential role, which you insist on with good reason. But it does not account for everything. For, there is also formal causality, and I fear that you have not taken sufficient account of its role.[11]

In addition to Eric McLuhan citing the influence of important philosophers on Marshall McLuhan's ideas, he attributed them as influencing his own theory regarding this key concept when asserting: "Formal causality is not something that can be abstracted, since it is always a dynamic relation between the user and the ever-changing situation."[12] This shows, once more, the relationship between Marshall McLuhan, Alfred Korzybski, and Aristotle.

Due to the importance of Eric McLuhan's ideas, I return to them in the following section.

---

10   Eric McLuhan in Letter dated May 28, 1969, unpublished. Maritain, along whit Etienne Gilson, had for some time been working and teaching at the Pontifical Institute for Medieval Studies, a few yards distance from McLuhan's office on the campus of St. Michael's College. Collegial conversations were not infrequent. See in McLuhan Marshall, McLuhan Eric. *Media and Formal Cause*. NeoPoiesis Press, LLC., Texas 2011, p. 2

11   Eric McLuhan in a letter written from Kolbsheim, dated August 10,1969, unpublished. In McLuhan Marshall, McLuhan Eric. *Media and Formal Cause*. NeoPoiesis Press, LLC., Texas 2011, p. 2

12   McLuhan Marshall, McLuhan Eric. *Media and Formal Cause*. NeoPoiesis Press, LLC., Texas 2011, p. 80

Analysis of Aristotle's and Marshall McLuhan's Theories of Formal Cause

Throughout this chapter, I will aim to demonstrate the importance of two authors who have made history based on their theories, particularly regarding the subject of causality. The first, Aristotle, developed the doctrine of the four causes with which he endeavored to explain reality as a whole. For him, this meant understanding humans, as well as the world in which they exist, since both are connected by common laws revealed by an in-depth analysis based on an examination of the four causes.

The second is Marshall McLuhan, who gained recognition in the middle of the twentieth century due to his theory on communication and its importance to the development of the individual, and thus, of society. Marshall McLuhan insists that media be studied as society's formal cause. Therefore, in this chapter, I shall explain Marshall McLuhan's view of formal cause based on philosophical concepts, in order to better understand his theory and offer a suitable interpretation of his thesis about media. Ergo, I also demonstrate how Marshall McLuhan links the above concept to the mediation between the individual and reality to construct his theory on media.

Formal Cause According to Aristotle

Born in Stagira circa 384-383 BC, Aristotle was a Greek philosopher whose father, Nicomachus, was a prominent physician in the service of Amyntas III, King of Macedon (and father of Philip II of Macedon). By the age of eighteen Aristotle was emancipated from his family and traveled to Athens, enrolling in Plato's Academy, where he stayed for twenty years. It is there that his thinking matured and where he established his own philosophical school of thought. During this time, he grasped the essence of the Platonic principles and argued them in several written works. Following Plato's death, Aristotle left the Academy to establish his own school in Athens, known as the Lyceum. Aristotle taught various philosophical disciplines while also dedicating himself to the study of natural science. In 323 BC, he left Athens for political reasons and withdrew to Chalcis, where he died in 322 BC following a few months of exile.

His body of work is divided into two main groups: exoteric writings in the form of dialogue designed for the general public, and esoteric work, targeted to his disciples, comprising the resource base of his didactic activity at the Lyceum and the school's internal heritage. The exoteric works have been almost completely lost; only some fragments and titles remain in existence. By contrast, his esoteric writings survived almost in full and deal with philosophical problems and questions in natural science. Some of these works, which relate to the subject in question herein, are among others: *Physics, On the Soul, Metaphysics, Nicomachean Ethics, Eudemian Ethics, Magna Moralia,* and *Parva Naturalia.*

Aristotle is of considerable significance to philosophy due to the abundance of his writings, their content, and his profound reflection therein. It is essential also to mention that his work focuses on certain key concepts in the understanding of reality, including but not limited to: substance, essence, actuality, and potentiality, as well as, of course, the four causes, all terms which are fundamental when attempting to analyze and understand the connection between humans and all that surrounds them, and specifically, society, as I expand upon below.

Aristotle used four concepts to analyze reality in areas such as Physics (what we can perceive with our senses), and Metaphysics (what we cannot perceive with our senses but rather with our intelligence). He asserts that things cannot be recognized as such without knowing their causes, meaning their material, formal, efficient, and final causes.

Although formal cause is the conceptualization central to this study, it is necessary to analyze the rest of the causes to comprehend and distinguish them.

The following analysis is based on two main texts: Aristotle's *Physics* and *Metaphysics*, two works that are fundamental for understanding the four causes. I shall also make use of some observations made by Thomas Aquinas on the same subject. His interpretation is important in order to appreciate the author and serves as a link that helps understand the current exegesis of the four causes used by subsequent authors such as, among others, Jacques Maritain, Étienne Gilson, and Marshall McLuhan. This dual analysis provides basic yet considerably useful information in order to consider both Marshall McLuhan's and Aristotle's visions in relation to this concept.

Aristotle begins his study with *Physics*, centering on the explanation of reality and, specifically, of motion. In this work, he alleged that knowledge of reality can only be achieved starting from what is most evident to us and moving towards that which is the least evident. This implies that to know the cause of a "thing," we must first know that "thing" that is most evident to us. Subsequently, in order to carry out a more objective examination of cause, he foregoes *Physics* and continues his explanation in *Metaphysics*, since evidently, the order of the causes belongs, strictly, to this work.

Thus, according to Aristotle, all of reality can be explained through the discovery of his four causes: "In one way, then, that out of which a thing comes to be and which persists, is called a cause, e.g., the bronze of the statue, the silver of the bowl, and the genera of which the bronze and the silver are species."[13] Therefore, this first definition pertains to what is tangible since the definition Aristotle offers us mentions, "that out of which a thing comes to be," meaning the bronze, which belongs to the recognized object and is the material out of which it is made. Without the bronze, there would be no bronze statue. Accordingly, it is one of its causes.

Regarding this kind of cause, Aristotle further suggests that language-wise, we can distinguish between what changes, meaning accidental properties of an object, and what does not, meaning substance in its primary sense: that is, form. Consequently, when we assert that "a thing becomes that from this" and not "this becoming that," we are mainly talking about things that do not survive the change. Meaning, things that are not necessary, as accidental properties are, such as when a person becomes educated from being uneducated, because what is contingent changes around the accidental properties or the qualities the material has due to it being changeable. On the other hand, though, change also occurs in things that survive (e.g. the form). We speak of a statue coming to be from bronze, not of the bronze becoming a statue.[14] Hence, material cause has to do in general with two kinds of change: 1) that which occurs accidentally and does not change the essence, such as what is educated and what is uneducated, and 2) that which is at the essence—bronze, when becoming a statue, preserves its material attributes, but changes its form. Another aspect that may be analyzed regarding accidental change is that which occurs in its own qualities or characteristics, in this case, the statue. And that may change. For example, shine. A statue can become shiny from opaqueness. However, if it did not have the opposing quality as a basis for the change, the shininess would not be a viable characteristic for said statue. In this sense, the emphasis given to this kind of "becoming" is contrariety since it may come to be from not being.

Conversely, in the case of formal change, the emphasis is not on the contrariety of the qualities, but on the underlying layer of being, for, "we find

---

13   *Physics*, 194b 24-26
14   *Physics*, 190a 21-25

in every case something that underlies from which proceeds that which comes to be; for instance (...) the statue from the bronze."[15] For change to happen, it is fundamental that such change of something, and that is the substratum, etymologically speaking, of what lies beneath. In Aristotle's example, the statue needs a material in which it can come to be, a substratum, a potential being to move towards from; that is the bronze.

According to Aristotle, the underlying nature can be known by analogy: the way bronze behaves in relation to the statue,[16] since before being a statue, the bronze was something amorphous (without the form of a statue). Be that as it may, how can something formless be known? How can inconceivable material cause something that "is"? One possible answer might be to reveal the primary thing holding the form of an object would be to "remove"[17] each part comprising its total. Thus, when eliminating affections, products, and potencies of bodies, what would remain as its substratum was matter, which can be recognized only once it united with form. Said otherwise, when the combination of matter and form comes to be, matter, which was "amorphous," is unknowable to humans. To that end, it could be known only via analogy. For this reason, Aristotle proposed that what "remained" after removal, if there was matter, was pure indeterminacy, or a certain non-being. Or as he noted in the treatise *On Generation and Corruption*, when discussing the transformation of elements, "Assuming, then, that the contrariety, in respect to which they are transformed, is one, the elements' will inevitably be two: for it is 'matter' that is the 'mean' between the two contraries, and matter is imperceptible and inseparable from them."[18] Since the importance of the second kind of cause (form), is one which orders matter to be what it is. Matter acquires "being," as such, from its combination with form. In this sense, Aristotle alleged that, "the species (idea), and what becomes of both (matter and species or form), seem to be more substance than matter."[19] And so, we may uphold that Aristotle's material cause is significant as a "principle" of being, since the substratum is the foundation on which change occurs. But as a "certain non-being" because it does not have an "entity" in itself, as such. This is why we can only know it or speak of it through analogy, otherwise it would be ontologically impossible to grasp. In summary, and strictly, matter "is" only through its union with form.

Subsequently, Aristotle refers to the second cause in objects: "In another

---

15 *Physics*, 190b 3-7
16 *Physics*, 191a 7-9
17 *Metaphysics*, 1029a 11-12
18 *GC II*, 5, 332a 32-35
19 *Metaphysics*, 1029a 29-30

way, the form or the archetype, i.e., the definition of the essence, and its genera, are called causes (e.g. the octave relation of 2:1, and generally, number), and the parts in a definition."[20] He spoke here of a second expression related to two different aspects; one is form, meaning the essence of the object in question (in this case, the statue), and the other aspect (the paradigm or the statue's shape).

According to Thomas Aquinas in his commentary on Aristotle's *Physics*, Aristotle distinguishes between two aspects of this second cause, due to different theories about the essence of things: "Plato said that the nature of species is certain abstract forms called examples or ideas, that is why he spoke of 'example' or 'paradigm.' On the other hand, philosophers of nature who spoke about form considered the forms in matter, therefore, they called it "species."[21]

Speaking about the "shape" of a thing is not too problematic, as we can refer to any object by noting whether it has a geometric or human form, and so forth. All the same, the subject of form in Aristotelian philosophy was highly complex because it referred not only to "one" of the causes of a thing, but to causes par excellence, which determined the thing to be what it was, meaning, it was thought to give a thing its essence.

As a result, Aristotle's formal cause implies two elements: essence and definition. On the one hand, essence actualizes the being's matter and determines it to be what it is. On the other hand, definition expresses what essence "is," meaning what being is. Both subjects refer to knowledge and cannot be dealt with in detail in the Aristotelian *Physics* treatise, since they focus more on the principles of being. That is why Aristotle provides a more detailed explanation of these in *Metaphysics*, in which he asserts that formal cause is the statement of essence and its genres.[22] As such, for him, formal cause is identical to the thing's essence of the thing, which is expressed through definition.

Throughout the Aristotelian analysis on form, the author gives an account of the need for the essence of the thing, for example, the bronze statue, to contain matter. The statue's form implies both its shape and the matter and form from which it is composed. In this way, formal cause "needs" certain elements that the statue's material cause contains. This means that the bronze statue would not be such without bronze. The statue would not be a statue without matter supporting it. Both material cause and formal cause necessarily belong to the being; they are both intrinsic to it.

The third kind of cause indicated by Aristotle is efficient cause, from which

---

20 *Physics,* 194b 26-29
21 Aquinas, Thomas. *Commentary on Aristotle's Physics.* Web. https://isidore.co/aquinas/Physics.htm
22 *Metaphysics,* 1013a 27-28

the primary source of change or rest comes: the human being who deliberated is a cause. For instance, parents are a child's cause, and generally, what makes is of what is made, and what changes is of what is changed.[23] This kind of cause has to do with something external to the subject which it moves or changes in some way. Likewise, this type of cause does not belong to the being since it does not move towards it, but is rather changed externally due to its own nature. To illustrate, Bronze does not naturally transform into a statue; it needs a sculptor to move it towards this determined form.

For Thomas Aquinas, this type of cause, especially, has four principal meanings:[24]

1) Perfective. The one which complements movement or change, introducing substantial form into production. This means that even though the subject or the being in question is already a thing in nature, given that the movement of its nature (matter and form) makes it what it is, the external agent moves that nature in order to artificially "generate" a modified substance.[25] It is a "modified substance" because its nature would have never led to such a transformation. Nevertheless, for Aquinas, it is perfective because when changing the being, it is given an artificial perfection different from the natural one, be it accidental or substantial. Accidental perfection refers to a change in any of the qualities of the subject in question. For example, if we say that, "Socrates is a musician," the quality perfecting Socrates is musicality. The other kind of perfection Aquinas speaks of is substantial. Here, he does not refer to accidental characteristics of the subject, but to its proper substance, for example, "the bronze statue." In this case, the bronze is perfected by the statue's "form" and, therefore, has a different definition than the fact that it is only bronze.

2) Preparative or dispositive. It is what prepares the matter or subject[26] for ultimate completion. According to this definition, matter, mean-

---

23   *Physics,* 194b 29-32
24   Aquinas, Thomas. *Commentary on Aristotle's Physics.* Web. https://isidore.co/aquinas/Physics.htm
25   In this case, the term refers to the composite of matter and form.
26   The term "subject," to which Thomas Aquinas refers is not very clear to me, as it can only refer to matter as substratum of change according to the exhaustive analysis of García Yebra in Aristóteles. *Metafísica* (translation and commentary of Valentín García Yebra), Gredos, Madrid 1998, p. XXXIV-XXXV (in Spanish). Or it may refer to substance as such when being shaped by matter and form. However, matter cannot be prepared for something artificial but rather be disposed for something else based on the actualization it gets from the form.

ing the substratum out of which change happens, is passive in relation to the change or modification that shall be made to it. Efficient cause is the active reason which actualizes matter's passivity or moves it towards action. This implies both elements indicated by Aquinas. On the one hand, the matter or subject are prepared for the change that efficient cause will carry out. And, on the other, they are disposed towards certain purposes according to their nature, that is, according to form.

3) Contributory. It is what does not operate for its own purpose but for the purpose of another. Efficient cause does not necessarily move the being towards its natural purpose, since this is up to formal cause, determining the matter and imbuing it with a specific essence. It rather moves it towards a different purpose. While the being's nature is "necessarily" disposed towards a purpose, it also "disposes" it towards multiple purposes. For example, wood is naturally wood, but its nature as wood disposes it to be moved by the carpenter to be a chair, or a table, and so forth. Thus, Aquinas noted that efficient cause does not operate towards its own (natural) purpose, but rather, towards the purpose of another (in this example, the carpenter's will).

4) Conceiving. In those operating for a purpose, it is that which gives the agent the form towards which he operates. The voluntary agent operates out of its own knowledge, which is provided by the counselor. In natural things, it is also said that the generator moves heavy or light objects in terms of giving them the form through which they move. In this sense, Aquinas demonstrates that efficient cause moves according to the form that the agent conceives. In the case of the wood and carpenter, the latter conceives of the form (a chair) that he shall give to the matter (wood). This is pertaining to things without consciousness. On a related note, conscious beings move according to the counseling of whoever generated said consciousness. For example, the carpenter's efficient cause would be whoever showed them what carpentry is, enabling them to move towards the occupation of carpenter. In this way, the subject's matter is "counseled" by the agent's form.

According to Aristotle, the last kind of cause is the goal, or purpose, i.e. the purpose of a stroll is health. Why does someone go on a stroll? We affirm: "to stay healthy," and in saying so, we are inferring an indication of causality (the stroll).²⁷ This kind of purpose implies essence because we can learn from it what a being is and where it is going. Relatedly, Aristotle claimed that the fact of "being human" implies that our final cause is happiness. But, in the case of artificial beings, humans are those who give them their purpose based on their essence. Case in point, the example of a chair, given that the carpenter decided that wood would take form of a chair, the purpose of its being is for people to sit on it. Furthermore, the artisan could modify its essence, and/or its purpose. For Thomas Aquinas, the explanation of this cause is evident since it answers a question like why one walks, we say: to be healthy. In responding as such, we reveal a cause and prove that the aim is cause no less than the others, even though it may seem likely, considering purpose is the last step in generation.²⁸ In relation to this last cause, it should be clarified that final cause does not only refer to the "ultimate purpose", but also to its intermediate purposes, since purpose is not last in absolute terms, but in relation to something.²⁹

After describing each cause, Aristotle noted that these abstractions are reductive and asserted that essence (formal cause) and purpose (final cause) are one, and that the primary source of motion is the same in these genera.³⁰ This is evidenced by the being's form "determining" what that being is, and said determination indicating the purpose towards which it is directed. If we consider humans we can identify at least two causes. We can say that their essence or formal cause is "being human," their purpose is to reach happiness (in Aristotelian terms), and that this is determined by their nature. In a suggested revision, Thomas Aquinas pointed out that the last three causes may be reduced to one: formal cause, given that they are all acts. Whereas, material cause is not of the same class, nor genera, as other causes because matter, as such, is a potential entity, due to the fact it needs form in order to "be." Meanwhile, it is a certain non-being.³¹ Logically, if it is true that there can be a certain reduction due to resemblance in some aspect of each one of the causes, this does not

---

27 *Physics*, 194b 32-35
28 Aquinas, Thomas. *Commentary on Aristotle's Physics*. Web. https://isidore.co/aquinas/Physics.htm
29 *Idem*
30 *Physics*, 198a 25-27
31 In order to understand what matter is, we need to remove each one of its attributes, such as size, form, amount, quantity, and so forth. What remains is matter, the substrate that holds each one of these attributes. But what is matter without attribute? Is it "pure" indetermination? It seems it cannot persist since there is nothing to determine it. For Aristotle, what "remains," if there is matter, is pure indetermination, or rather a certain non-being which couldn't not be, as it would be nothing and would not be disposed to receive form nor become a being as such since it is undetermined, it is pure potentiality. Some additional problematics around this idea are noted by Bostock, see *Metaphysics: Books Z and H*, translated with a commentary by David Bostock, p. 77.

imply that one is the same as the other. Regardless, Aristotle's classification demonstrated that each one had a different purpose in the being. Each one of the four is its cause.

Formal Cause According to Marshall McLuhan

Marshall McLuhan, an acknowledged communication theorist since the 1960s, put media studies on the academic map. During his life, he was a highly criticized, but prophetic media scholar, who's works prophetically envisioned media studies as a transformative academic subject well before the digital and algorithmic age. According to Lance Strate,[32] one of McLuhan's most significant contributions is the rhetorical invention of *the media* as a term and category in public discourse. Before Marshall McLuhan, there were many other academic, activist, and artistic interpretations and exhibitions inspired by broad extensions of our senses, including but not limited to: entertainment, public address, technologies and techniques, symbols, codes, and all other mass media and cultural formations. Within his canonical text, *Understanding Media* (1964), McLuhan highlighted topics like the analysis of speech, writing, bicycles, electricity, the telephone, clothing, and more reframing them as *medias*. In addition, he demonstrated how the hidden space separating humans from reality unites each of these elements that were seen before as separate and even opposite of each other. He showed that language *is* technology, that tools and machines *are* forms of communication, and all our technological extensions are *media*.

McLuhan began his higher education studying at the University of Manitoba from 1928 until 1934, majoring in English Literature. Subsequently, he earned a second master's degree and a Ph.D. from the University of Cambridge in rhetoric, grammar, and dialectic subjects. There, he studied under I.A. Richards, who greatly influenced his thought, as the latter's main interest was language from a psychological point of view. Richards attempted late in his work to construct a science of criticism, examining how literature produces certain psychological states. In *The Meaning of Meaning* (1923), Richards proclaimed that grammar and language are not independent of the subjects using them. Marshall McLuhan expanded on this significantly, given that language is a medium par excellence and is central in the explanation of other communication tools.

For I. A. Richards, words in themselves mean nothing. Their meaning

---
32 Strate L., Wachtel E. "Media Trascendence", *The Legacy of McLuhan*. Hampton Press, Inc. New Jersey, 2005

depends on the ways they are used. According to him, only when a thinking being makes use of them do they represent something or have meaning. They are tools. Therefore, they are controlled by thought which determines their meaning depending on the context.[33] This idea was later expanded further by Marshall McLuhan.

In 1937, McLuhan began teaching at the English Department of St. Louis University. There, he supervised Walter Ong's MA thesis and began familiarizing himself with Thomas Aquinas's philosophy. Later on, he would self-identify as a Thomist.

Among his most significant influences, and in respect of this theory, are several Neo-Thomists, such as J. Owens, Étienne Gilson, Jacques Maritain, and others, as demonstrated by the reference he made to them in a variety of his writings, as well as in personal correspondences:

> Only yesterday, I was reading a chapter on "Judgment and Truth in Aquinas" by my friend, Fr. Owens, here at the Medieval Institute. He concludes: 'They involve the traditional Aristotelian view that the cognitive agent is and becomes the thing known (...) Its structure comes from the thing known, and not from any a priori in the intellect'. (...) It turns out then that my communication theory is Thomistic to the core. It has the further advantage of being able to explain Aquinas and Aristotle in modern terms. We are the content of anything we use, if only because these things are extensions of ourselves. The meaning of the pencil or the chair I use is the interplay between me and these things. Again, the message of these things is the sum of the changes that result from their social use. Thus, I have added two features to 'the medium is the message,' namely the content and the meaning.[34]

These references demonstrate Marshall McLuhan's in-depth reflections regarding society and the media, as well as his interest in ancient philosophy, especially Aristotelian theory, its relation to medieval philosophy, and strictly speaking, to that of Thomas Aquinas.

Afterwards, McLuhan taught at Assumption College in Windsor, Ontario. And, lastly, at the University of Toronto's St. Michael's College, where he spent the rest of his career except for one year (1967-1968) at Fordham University. During the 1950s, while teaching at the University of Toronto, he became

---

33   See: Hernández Juan Abelardo. *Rationality in Marshall McLuhan and the Toronto School*. Doctoral thesis, Universidad Panamericana, 2004, p. 11 (in Spanish)

34   See: McLuhan Marshall, McLuhan Eric. *Media and Formal Cause*. NeoPoiesis Press, Texas 2011, p. 6

acquainted with Harold Innis, a professor of political economy who later in his career researched communication subjects and influenced McLuhan to focus on the media.

Innis's research focused on the social history of communication media. He believed that the relative stability of different cultures depends on the balance and proportion of their media. For Innis, the key to social change is found in the development of media, and each medium embodies a bias[35] in terms of organization and control of information. Any empire or society relates, generally speaking, to time duration and an expansion over space. In addition, Innis was convinced that stable societies were those that found a balance between time and space *biases*. He believed that change originated in the margins of society since marginalized people invariably develop their own media. For Innis, new media enabled those on the sidelines to develop and consolidate power, and ultimately, change central authority. Concurrently, he viewed oral communication, speech, as a time-based bias since it requires a relatively ephemeral means of contact. Historically speaking, spoken knowledge depended upon a line of transmission that was often associated with ancestors and seemingly immediate contact. Finally, Innis asserted that speech was more flexible and humanistic than the written word, which was rigid and impersonal.[36]

Thus, during his explorations of communication, Innis observed an operative principle of the philosophy of history: the idea that one's thoughts form dependently as they, too, develop over time. Ironically, time did not allow him to develop these ideas further. Instead, his most prominent disciple, Marshall McLuhan, took from Innis's theories a series of tools with which he broadened into an aesthetic doctrine, developing them into his own exhaustive theories of social change.[37]

---

35   This term, created by Innis and referring to a certain type of communication media, is important. It is used today regularly in American and Canadian communication language. According to Innis's research, the media, or bias, have influenced different societies throughout history, meaning changes that happen in different cultures can be explained via at least two biases: the first relates to time-biased media, such as stone and clay, which are durable and heavy. Because they are difficult to move, they do not imply territorial expansion. Nevertheless, having a long life, they foment an extension of the empire throughout time. Innis associated these media with the customary, the sacred, and the moral. The bias of time facilitates the development of social hierarchies, ancient Egypt being the paradigm. For Innis, speech is a time-biased medium. The second bias relates to space, with what is light and portable. These may be transported over long distances. The example is paper, which as a medium that can be easily transported even though its lifespan is relatively short. Web. May 15, 2013, http://www.media-studies.ca/articles/innis.htm

36   Web. May 15, 2013, http://www.media-studies.ca/articles/innis.htm

37   See: Hernández Juan Abelardo. *Rationality in Marshall McLuhan and the Toronto School*. Doctoral thesis, Universidad Panamericana, 2004, p. 25 (in Spanish)

Harold Innis, who was the first to study the effects of mass media, described how writing on paper instead of on stone revolutionized human history. Militarism originates in papyrus because the latter facilitated sending messages. The fall of the Roman Empire happened once papyrus dried up. What Innis did not know, was that the papyrus of the Nile dried up because the Romans contaminated the river.[38]

While it is true that Marshall McLuhan was influenced by some canonical thinkers of his time, it should also be noted that he differentiated himself from whatever he did not deem coherent with his theory, as shown in the above quote. In addition, he synthesized the knowledge acquired from of his predecessors to develop new theories, engendering himself as a *media guru*, or the *oracle of the electronic age*, according to his most loyal followers and experts in communication.[39]

Throughout his lifetime, Marshall McLuhan demonstrated the importance of media[40] to society and to the development and conduct of humans in it. He knew media permeated all that we do, that they are in/of the world and part of our lives. Thus, they catalyze changes, altering our experiences.

---

38   McLuhan Marshall. "Teoría de la imagen", *Salvat*, Salvat Editores, Barcelona 1973, p. 8-23 (in Spanish)

39   I referred to Lance Strate who is Professor of Communication and Media Studies at Fordham University, and has previously served as Department Chair, Associate Chair for Graduate Studies, Associate Chair for Undergraduate Studies, and Program Director for the Professional Studies in New Media major he developed for Fordham's School of Professional and Continuing Studies. He held the Harron Family Endowed Chair in Communication at Villanova University in 2015 as a visiting professor and was given an honorary appointment as Chair Professor at Henan University in Kaifeng, China in 2016. Lance Strate is internationally recognized for his scholarship, intellectual leadership, and creative activities. He is currently engaged in several research projects including an examination of the relationship between time and technology, a theoretical investigation of semantic ecology; an overview of the evolution of media environments, and a philosophical study of Marshall McLuhan. Lance Strate is currently President of the Institute of General Semantics, having previously served as the IGS Executive Director, he is the founder of the Media Ecology Association, and served as MEA President for over a decade. He is also Past President of New York State Communication Association, the New York Society for General Semantics, and currently Co-Chair of the Global Listening Centre's Academic Board. https://www.fordham.edu/info/29829/cms_faculty_and_staff/4882/lance_strate

40   Hereinafter, we shall use the term *media* according to how Marshall McLuhan understood it, and as explained above.

The Relationship Between Formal Cause and Media

Thanks to his background in history and communication, Marshall McLuhan took immense interest in societal formations during his lifetime. He saw media not only as tools utilized in various ways, but also as parts of our environment. In other words, McLuhan knew we are influenced by mediums in every situation, even in moments when they are taken for granted due to dominant hegemonic norms that permeate all spheres of our lives, configuring our being in space and time.

With this, it may be asserted that humans are "conditioned" entities, since each thing they come into contact with eventually becomes a condition of their existence, be it family life, institutions they belong to, friends, and/or the media informing their relationships within a society. To be clear, a comprehensive understanding of life cannot be understood in isolation. Along these lines, to grasp ancient Greek, Roman, or any other culture that one may wish to analyze, they must first learn its context, circumstances, and atmosphere in which it operated, garnering a fuller picture of truth about a society during a specific moment. Again, human beings are holistically shaped by their environment. Perhaps even more so than animals, since it is believed by some figures in certain cultures that the latter's lives are more profoundly conditioned by biology. In constrast, human life is said to be lesser conditioned, since we are willfully capable of separating ourselves from biological needs to conscientiously achieve a determined objective or goal. For example, some people decide not to eat certain foods for different reasons or because they wish to achieve a certain shape. As far as we know, this does not happen in animals, despite their environment, their society, and their medias. On the contrary, it has been argued that they seek to satisfy their needs at whatever cost, guided primarily by a desire to fulfill their biological aims.

Furthermore, humans can intervene in whatever conditions them. According to Hannah Arendt, "the things that owe their existence exclusively to men nevertheless constantly condition their human makers," meaning, "men constantly create their own, self-made conditions."[41] For Marshall McLuhan, these conditions were deeply connected to media, since humans are interconnected by relationships, dialogue, and other internal and external conditions, comprising each organism and their surroundings. Hence, any changes introduced into an environment systematically influence our lives. And, resultingly, we are shaped by each medium differently:

---

41   Web. May 8, 2013 https://hac.bard.edu/amor-mundi/we-create-the-conditions-that-condition-us-2012-05-28

> The new medium of TV as an environment creates new occupations. (...) But the effects of TV on the movie go unnoticed, and the effects of the TV environment in altering the entire character of human sensibility and sensory ratios is completely ignored.[42]

Although more obvious to us now in the algorithmic age, McLuhan's perspective was a novel one. For him, the diversity of media shaped our being, meaning they reveal to us a previously naturalized essence of humanity. Said otherwise, twentieth-century humans are not the same as those of the fifth, and to a large extent due to the technological and rational progress caused by medias. We could, of course, debate whether humans have truly advanced, rationally speaking, throughout the centuries. Or whether the technological development of rationality capacity helped humans become progressively more human. For instance, several media scholars have documented detriments to faculties, like memory, as a result of new media usage. Nevertheless, this critique is not the central focus of this manuscript: the influence of media. The truth is, "we are other human beings" with the same essence, besides enacting unique identities and, more concretely, as a body.

It is in this sense that Marshall McLuhan proclaimed that the media of his age and all of history were society's formal cause due to the fact they changed people in a fundamental ways, conditioning us. McLuhan spoke to this when he said:

> Formal cause is the causality of emergent properties, the causality that media ecologists often have in mind when we consider the impact of technological change on the individuals and societies, on communication, consciousness, and culture.[43]

Let us analyze this assertion from an Aristotelian point of view. It does not seem clear that formal cause is an emergent cause because, for Aristotle, formal cause determined the being's essence inasmuch as "it is what it is." Remember, Aristotle's formal cause did not change easily, it did not "emerge," but rather remained throughout the being's movement and ensured that despite changes, the being continued being "what it is." What does change is the matter that

---

42 See McLuhan Marshall, McLuhan Eric. *Media and Formal Cause*. NeoPoiesis Press, Texas 2011, p. 2

43 See: Lance Strate in McLuhan Marshall, McLuhan Eric. *Media and Formal Cause*. NeoPoiesis Press, LLC., Texas 2011, p. X

formed the being, together with its accidental characteristics. However, we can expand this assertion from two different points of view. First, by referring to formal cause in the medium this way. For example, a television's formal cause would be its definition: that which transmits remote images via electromagnetic waves. To qualify as a television, several necessary elements of an object must be found according to the definition of a TV, otherwise, it would not be deemed a television. However, if the television's color changes, or if it was scratched, or a frame was placed in it, it would not cease to be what it is. Now, if this item was used differently, i.e. instead being used as a projector, it was used to place plates, drinking glasses, and all that is needed to eat, then it would no longer be a TV, but most likely a table. Form here would indeed be affected, accidentally, due to the use of a tool. Thus, the definition of a thing changes via (mis)use, as does its perceived form.

Secondly, we can analyze how form is capable of change using a hypothetical of an individual who uses media for various actions. Case in point, when humans interact with the realities surrounding them, they use tools that allow them to distinguish, change, and manifest themselves. This tool usage changes humans as well, accidentally, as they continue to be "what they are," but their traits vary in such a way that an extreme change in humans is possible. Speaking to this sentiment, McLuhan asserted: "Any extension [...] whether of skin, hand, or foot, affects the whole physic and social complex."[44] Because of its relevance, this subject will be elaborated on in the following chapter.

Due to this influence on society, for Marshall McLuhan formal cause was synonymous to media in various ways. For instance, around 1964, he identified the concept as a cause of internal and social change in humans.[45] Similarly, numerous other canonical scholars denoted media's influence. To quote a number from the nineteenth century: Henry David Thoreau provoked, "We do not ride on the railroad; it rides upon us," Mark Twain wrote, "if all you have is a hammer, everything looks like a nail," and lastly, Winston Churchill said, "we shape our buildings, and thereafter they shape us." Dominant archetypes of progress influence humans, and to a certain degree, even surpasses them, as they cease to be the technology's owners and become their slaves.

Ultimately, it must be said that the conditions we create are used as shields against inherited conditions. That is to say, we negate what came before, creating something new which in some way was already in the past, since all that emerges as new has what was before at its roots. Thus, these new human created conditions are placed between us and what we consider the environment. Our conditions act as mediums between us and our actions, which is the same

---

44 Ibid p. 2
45 Ibid p. 1

as stating that our conditions are human life's media. Therefore, Marshall McLuhan insisted, "...our human senses, of which all media are extensions, [...] configure the awareness and experience of each one of us..."[46] In addition, a moment arises in this mediation in which the conditions created by humans ultimately form part of the atmosphere around them and become their own environment. Being part of our media, they become routine, rendering the conditions we created invisible to ourselves.

Today, this is clear, as we notice we are "used to" using certain tools in our daily lives without giving a thought to their existence, many of them being inherited conditions. While the tools and conditions found in our environment, form part of inherited conditions, as time goes on we no longer see them as a mediations but rather as extensions of ourselves capable of being manipulated to attain our aims. This is a process not necessarily born from the natural environment, but potentially from yet another perceived deficiency. Therefore, and as Arendt asserts:

> Whatever touches or enters into a sustained relationship with human life immediately assumes the character of a condition of human existence. This is why men, no matter what they do, are always conditioned beings.[47]

Marshall McLuhan thoroughly developed this question as he examined the impact media has on humans. In his eyes, media have such an effect that they can be said to essentially alter and conditioning us, in the way Arendt indicated above. Thus, media made by humans in societies are a formal cause of our change. Namely, our essence is accidentally modified by this dependence on the media we continuously use to develop in this world. Just as Aristotle asserted in his time, humans' essence has a certain "relation" to some of their accidents. In this case, proper accidents,[48] and said accidents may originate

---

46   McLuhan Marshall. *Understanding Media: the Extensions of Man*. MIT Press, London 1994, p. 11
47   Web. May 8, 2013 https://hac.bard.edu/amor-mundi/we-create-the-conditions-that-condition-us-2012-05-28
48   The distinction between proper accidents and accidental ones arises from analyzing visible substance, since it is itself also mobile, continuously passing from one state to another. For example, from being uneducated to educated. At first glance, this is substance in a certain state, meaning together with its accidents, as if what moves from being uneducated to educated were, let us suppose, the White human being, also determined by all of the other accidents which characterize the state from which change comes. However, this is not so because what passes from being uneducated to educated is not the White human, but simply a human, with "white" having to do with the accident of a substance at a certain moment. Humans are the ones changing from one state to another. Therefore, what changes

from the relationship between humans and any one environment.

As discussed, Marshall McLuhan's focal point was humans, their relations, and concepts of reality. Societally, as human life progresses, we are formed by relationships, initially with those around us, and later, with via media we utilize during interactions. Thus: "Society is not given, according to McLuhan. Media create social environments."[49] McLuhan emphasized this interaction's mediation, which for him, as explained above, was a determining factor of the individual, and more generally, society. The essence of a subject is affected since, as detailed, the essence of humans implies accidentalities, but does not necessitate that the essence itself changes.

Thus, media form part of the environment. They are something in themselves, as they do not depend on humans or on reality to be what they are as objects. In this view, media include words, language, highways, numbers, clothing, money, photography, and so forth. Each of them has a being that influences humans differently due to the kind of media they "are" in them. Also, the relationship a person has with any one media type will be different because each one can be used in a multitude of ways and for various actions. This was also the perspective of Marshall McLuhan who often designated media as "forms" of change, as they determine the information being transmitted and essentially modify the sender and receiver. And when seen through this lens, media(s) can be viewed as a society's formal cause. Next, I overview a short analysis of some of the most prominent media(s) for humanity, and how they influenced the formation of human lives.

To reiterate, many effects of media often lie outside of societal and individual attention. According to Marshall McLuhan, the only thing we perceive is the content of the information. However, he asserted, regardless of a lack of recognition, mediums have remain dominant forces, provoking the most significant changes in human behavior. As he remarked in an interview for the Salvat Library in 1973, "Societies have always been more conditioned by the nature of their mass media than by the message they transmit." Accordingly, what most impacts a society that receives any kind of information is the means by which it is informed. Reading a newspaper is not the same as listening to the radio; information is received according to the "form" in which it is

---

is also the only thing that remains, as substance is modified but does not change; accidents do not change, but they rather emerge or disappear. What changes is the substance. In this way, the distinction between contingent accidents in substance and accidental ones is noted. The change and what remains throughout the change is necessary or contingent. See: Inciarte Fernando. *Tiempo, sustancia, lenguaje: ensayos de metafísica.* p. 24 (in Spanish).

49 Macmillan Robert. "Marshall McLuhan at the Mercy of His Commentators", *Philosophy of the Social Sciences.* 1992; 22; 475. Web. http//pos.sagepub.com.

contained. Without this form, the message would not be what it is; it would be untransmittable.

Changes in society are not only due to changes of an era, but also due to something deeper generating radical changes in the rationality of humans. These changes are definitively linked to the media and their influence on society considering every individual needs to use technologies like, means of communication, transportation, and so on. Their influences does not only permeate and reshape human relations, but they also metamorphose the entire environment in/of which human beings exist over the life course. Ergo, mediums influence us both directly and indirectly.

After Marshall McLuhan elucidated the consequences of media on our ever evolving social relations, he analyzed the types of causation in mediums themselves that bring about these changes. As one might expect, his research was based upon Aristotle's four causes, reviewed above. Hence, closer examination of Aristotle leads to a better understanding of McLuhan's media theories. In a letter addressed to the twentieth century Neo-Thomist Jacques Maritain, he wrote:

> I am quite aware that nobody has attempted to understand metamorphosis and causality in social institutions through a minute inspection of the sensory and perceptual changes resulting from the new environments. Surely the history of philosophy can never be written without a complete awareness of these matters.

To which Maritain replied:

> I am overall in agreement with what you have written to me (...) This, in its way, plays an essential role, which you insist on with good reason. But it does not account for everything. For, there is also formal causality, and I fear that you have not taken sufficient account of its role.[50]

Following the suggestion of Maritain—who was influenced by Aristotelianism, but focused more on Thomas Aquinas, mainly due to his closeness to Catholicism—Marshall McLuhan focused his attention on formal cause. Aquinas's suggestion also correlated to the changes that media bring

---

50   A letter addressed to Jacques Maritain from May 28, 1969, which is unpublished. See: McLuhan Marshall, McLuhan Eric. *Media and Formal Cause*. NeoPoiesis Press, Texas 2011, p. 4. Together with Étienne Gilson, Jacques Maritain carried out research and taught for some time at the Pontifical Institute for Medieval Studies, which was located at a short distance from Marshall McLuhan's office at the St. Michael's College campus. According to the latter's son, Eric McLuhan, their conversations were frequent.

about in society. Once more, this is because "form" is what configures matter in order to constitute an object. Thanks to form, content is determined, and the latter may be communicated, only as long as it has a medium, a way by which it may be disseminated. To better understand this concept of McLuhan, we may also refer to Aristotelian Hylomorphism. In short, Hylomorphism is a theory Aristotle adapted to emphasize that reality is made of both form and matter, where a) matter: underlies, changes, and individualizes the being, and b) form: "determines" what matter is, gives it its essence; its being. In that case, a medium is said to determine form of media, and the content or information conveyed is its matter. As shown, a medium–message/form–matter analogy clarifies Marshall McLuhan's concept regarding media.

A second way of looking at form from Marshall McLuhan's media ecological perspective can be added. Firstly, we saw that society is significantly affected by the influence media has on it. In other words, we take for granted using media(s) for our day-to-day tasks, and by proxy of this naturalization, the ways we depend on them recede out of our view. This naturalizing process is in fact how media modify our actions and thinking, and how they part and parcel accidentally "affect" our essence. Secondly, and due to Maritain's influence, form is designated anew. This time, however, as a determiner of the "message" because form is the medium carrying information; therefore, it determines what is said. As we shall see below, this is evidenced by information not being the same, for example, in text, image(s), and/or via words said aloud. Although the content being sent is the same, the message may be received differently according to the medium utilized.

Moreover, as I formerly mentioned, I have found no concerted efforts being made to explore causes of social change in this fashion, or at least not in proper philosophical terms. Despite this, I have demonstrated the relation between the effects of communication and Aristotelian cause theory, and how it provoked a significant change in Marshall McLuhan's analysis, i.e., their focuses on formal cause and its influence on environment. Said otherwise, McLuhan purported that media must be studied as "forms," and as means that create new ideas and point at novel objectives.[51] The change in paradigm that he presented in this way was transformational. McLuhan focused attention not on the content being conveyed, but on the form that determines what is transmitted. Against odds, he inferred that which makes a thing a thing is part of the message being emitted, or rather "is" the message itself: "the effect of media, like their "message," is really contributed to form and not to content."[52]

---

51 McLuhan E., Zingrone F. *Essential McLuhan*. Anansi, Toronto 1995, p. 187
52 McLuhan Marshall. "Myth and Mass Media" in *Daedalus*, Vol. 88, No. 2, Myth and Mythmaking (spring 1959), MIT Press, p. 342

This claim is determinant in understanding what influence the medium has within societies. His emphasis was placed on the medium's form; confident this is what to focus on in communication. Lesser so on the content because, at the end of the day, form is what determines the information, or rather, in Aristotelian terms, the matter.

In kind, formal cause for Marshall McLuhan was, in multiple senses, synonymous with the medium. Towards 1964, he identified media as the cause for changes in societal reasoning. Apart from media exercising pervasive pressures on the environment without overt recognition, media perpetuate taken for granted formal cause in societies. Therefore, McLuhan stated in his *Letters*:

> (Frederick Whilhelmsen) is interested in working on St. Thomas's theory of communication, and I have pointed out to him that Aquinas designates his audience, the people he wants to influence and alter, in the Objections of each article. Then I realized that the audience is, in all matters of art and expression, the formal cause, e.g., fallen man is the formal cause of the Incarnation, and Plato's public is the formal cause of his philosophy. Formal cause is concerned with effects and with structural form, and not with value judgments.
>
> My own approach to the media has been entirely from formal cause. Since formal causes are hidden and environmental, they exert their structural pressure by interval and interface with whatever is in their environmental territory. Formal cause(s are) always hidden, whereas the things upon which they act are visible. The TV generation has been shaped not by TV programs, but by the pervasive and penetrating character of the TV image, or service, itself.[53]

As exhibited above, McLuhan considered the media as formal cause of change in humans due to their influence on the environment, and despite human inability to notice. What is of key interest is that media carry information; therefore, that is what should matter most to humans. The information is not what changes us as a society. It is the media we live with every day that does.

This idea is expressed in a number of McLuhan's works. One of the most important ones, due to the influence it had on the field of communication, and considered by some as holy scripture, making Marshall McLuhan the first oracle of his time,[54] is *Understanding Media: The Extensions of Man*. In

---

53 McLuhan Marshall, McLuhan Eric. *Media and Formal Cause*. NeoPoiesis Press, LLC., Texas 2011, p. 130

54 So asserted by Lewis H. Lapham, in the introduction to McLUHAN Marshall, *Understanding Media: The Extensions of Man*, MIT Press, London 1994

it, he proclaimed that "We become what we behold. [...] We shape our tools and then our tools shape us."⁵⁵ The media we perceive, and through which we communicate, transform our messages in a determined way. Communication has changed over time. Media has changed; the humans of oral tradition are not the same as those of literary tradition. According to McLuhan, our tools have made us who we are:

> The railway did not introduce movement or transportation or wheel or road into human society, but it accelerated and enlarged the scale of previous human functions, creating totally new kinds of cities and new kinds of work and leisure. This happened whether the railway functioned in a tropical or a northern environment, and is quite independent of the freight or content of the railway medium.⁵⁶

For Marshall McLuhan, the Media,⁵⁷ of which one major example was the railway, caused changes that catalyzed further than its surface level purpose and function. Practically, the form of a railway system implicates changes in the environment, in reality, in society. The introduction of the railway increased our speed in bodily movement and information, impacting everything else.

Before expanding on the sheer impact of the medium on society-building, I must first discuss what McLuhan meant by media, to better acknowledge his theory regarding formal cause.

The term "medium" may be defined in several ways;⁵⁸ one way to understand this concept is as an environment, or atmosphere, arising from the relation between humans and the world. As thoroughly detailed, the way humans behave depends on media. Another way is to think of media as conduits or vehicles, something that links two points. In this sense, media(s) connect humans and reality, as we are always seeking ways to relate to our surroundings. A third way medium has been defined is as, "a substance that surrounds or impregnates what goes between two points, not by drawing or tracing a line between

---

55   *Ibidem*
56   McLuhan Marshall, McLuhan Eric. *Media and Formal Cause*. NeoPoiesis Press, Texas 2011, p. 1
57   Marshall McLuhan's work, *Understanding Media*, introduces concepts such as *Media*, and *Global Village* into language for the first time, which shall become key both for the development of his work as of communication theory. See: McLuhan Marshall. *Understanding Media: The Extensions of Man*. MIT Press, London 1994, p. 10
58   I take this information from Lance. A. Strate, Professor of Communication and Media Studies and Associate Chair for Graduate Studies. B.S., Cornell University; M.A., Queens College, City University of New York, Ph.D. New York University. See: Strate A. Lance. "Studying Media As Media: McLuhan and the Media Ecology Approach", *Media Tropes eJournal*, Vol. 1 (2008) p. 134

them, but by drawing a circle around them." For example, fish swim through the medium which is water, same as we move through air. Some bacteria live in mediums, such as milk, transforming it into yogurt. We call that colony a culture. Likewise, cultures are formed within mediums. Mediums are not produced by cultures.[59] Understanding this necessitates a change of paradigm, since it is more commonly believed that media arise from societal and cultural developments; its rationality. However, what is often not taken into account is that the tools we build permeate the realities in which we develop, mediating our actions, and determining the ways what we see and do. We unfold in reality through media, and the influence they have on us is a crucial component of our experiences.

According to Lance Strate, media are not like billiard balls which produce effects when hitting other balls. They are more like the table on which the game is played. In this, the medium is not "an actor," but "the stage" on which humans play their roles. In addition, as environments, the media do not determine our actions, but rather limit the range of possibilities of human action.[60] Consequently, media are the conditioning factors of many human actions. Although they do not determine in an absolutist way due to their freedom, users of media are inclined in certain ways, and towards certain paths. Therefore, we may say that the media direct a large percentage of human action. This is why an analysis of their impact on different societies is profoundly significant.

Media function as environments, ecologies, and/or systems. On the other hand, content is what happens within the system and may, or not, affect it. Thus, for Marshall McLuhan, the medium is more significant than the content, the message, or in other words, the form. For him the medium, or form, is more important since it determines what the content, or matter, becomes.

Finally, in regard to media, these are for Marshall McLuhan environments or surroundings. These do not refer only to mass media,[61] but also include any technologies that create extensions of the human body and senses. From the clothes we wear to the computer or whatever technological means we use, since he viewed society as being more conditioned by the nurture of its media than by the message itself. It has been believe that from the outset, humans have used "media" to function in the naturally inhospitable environments that surrounded them. Further, by adapting in this way, we incrementally achieved consolidation of tribes, and thereafter, societies from which culture and customs emerged. Any extension of humans, be it skin, hands, or feet, are media that affect them both socially and psychologically. This is Marshall McLuhan's interest; using

---

59   *Ibid*, p. 135
60   *Idem*
61   Means of communication intended to reach the masses.

this point of view to understand the technological environment and its impact on humans.

That is why the main theme of his theory was about the media, and as he pronounced in his interview with Playboy magazine,[62] as extensions of humans, media changes them in profound internal and external ways. He continued on to state that the environment in which they develop changes in a multitude of ways refashioning their means of communication and use of extensions.

McLuhan insisted that every extension, or medium, is an intensification and amplification of an organ, sense, or function, wherever it occurs. He expressed that humans are easily fascinated by any material, other than themselves, that extends them, be it the telephone for the ears, the television for the eyes, and so forth. For many physiological reasons, our extensions of ourselves induce a state of numbness; according to Marshall McLuhan, extensions are those that provoke this state. Medical researchers such as Hans Selye and Adolphe Jonas maintain that all our extensions, in sickness and in health, are attempts to maintain equilibrium. McLuhan also believed that any extension of the being causes a self-amputation. The body uses this power or strategy of self-amputation when its perceptual power is unable to locate or avoid the cause of irritation.[63]

For instance, in cases of physical stress due to different types of excessive stimuli, the central nervous system protects itself using a strategy of amputation or isolation of the offending organ, sense, or function. Thus, the stimulus to an invention is the stress of an accelerated pace and increase of load. Furthermore, in the case of the wheel, as an extension of the foot, the pressure of the consequent burdens of the accelerated exchange of monetary and/or written media(s) was an immediate impetus for the desired extension and amputation of this function from the body.[64]

According to Lance Strate, these amputations occur because of the media. Our media "numbs" our body and mind;[65] e.g., the process of writing. It revolutionized no need to memorize, as everything was recorded in a book to access as needed. As follows, Marshall McLuhan claimed that any extension is also a self-amputation, being that every medium we use numbs and "outdates" previous abilities. Alternatively, as Max Frisch avowed in his novel *Homo Faber*, "technology is the knack of so arranging the world that we

---

62   See: McLuhan Eric, Zingrone Frank. *Essential McLuhan*. Anansi, Toronto 1995, p. 237
63   McLuhan Marshall. *Understanding Media: The Extensions of Man*. MIT Press, London 1994, p. 52
64   *Ibid* p. 53
65   See: Strate A. Lance. "Studying Media As Media: McLuhan and the Media Ecology Approach". *Media Tropes eJournal*, Vol. 1 (2008) p. 127-142

don't have to experience it,"⁶⁶ for it seems humans develop in the world from their "media," which implies extensions of themselves that are intermediaries between humanity and worldliness. Again, it is important to remember that for McLuhan, media were not only those advances that come from technology or the world's artificiality, but also the arms, the hands, and skin that are all a bodily extension of human capacities. We could then ask ourselves, what were humans to Marshall McLuhan? If, to him, each part of us was an extension, a problem arises in humans' essence or definition. However, this study's topic focuses on media. It will, therefore, suffice to point out this matter for a future project.

For these reasons, it was not out of the ordinary for McLuhan to speak of "extensions" when referring to either the biological world and/or the technologically artificial, or simulated, ones. For others, technology is not exclusively human, as we may notice in beavers' dams, birds' nests, anthills, beehives, and other far more elaborate structures where technology is present in the animal world.⁶⁷ Technology is not only an extension of humans but also of nature. Living beings adapt to their environment through the tools, be it extrinsic or intrinsic, that nature provides them, and both serve as extensions, or media, that allow them to develop in the world in order to survive.

Therefore, one may assert that the human body is our first medium, as we are born with it and develop from it. Perhaps that is why Lewis Mumford said that the first machines were made of flesh and blood and appeared in antiquity.⁶⁸ Reminiscent of McLuhan stating, the "media" are not bridges between humans and nature; they "are nature." Media are not alien to humans but rather part of their world and reality. They cannot develop without them. How would humans be able to make tools without their hands, which are themselves a medium, or communicate with others without language, which is yet another medium, and in turn comes from other media, e.g., the mouth and the vocal cords? It is not difficult to say what a medium is; it is rather difficult to say what it is not. Distinguishing humans from their media was challenging even for Marshall McLuhan because the human body was a tool, but also an essential part of each human being. Hence the relevance of formal cause, since form is what defines or gives essence to matter. In this case, humans "are what they are" due to their

---

66   Frisch Max. *Homo Faber: A Report* (M. Bullock, trans.). Harcourt, Inc., San Diego 1959, p. 178

67   Mumford Lewis. *Art and technics*. Columbia University Press, New York, 1952 in STRATE A. Lance, "Studying Media As Media: McLuhan and the Media Ecology Approach" *Media Tropes eJournal*, Vol. 1 (2008) p. 136

68   Mumford Lewis. *The myth of the machine: 1. Technics and human development*. Harcourt, New York, 1967 in Strate A. Lance. "Studying Media As Media: McLuhan and the Media Ecology Approach", *Media Tropes eJournal*, Vol. 1 (2008) p. 136

form; they act, think, and feel as humans because form determines, to a certain extent, their capabilities, while their freedom determines another part. For this reason, we cannot say that the media, the means of communication, determine us in an absolute way, as this would be tantamount to negating the freedom that humanity itself implies.

Realistically, media transform our environment, and this impacts us. The way we perceive reality differs according to the media we use to capture it. Being acquainted with reality through a book or by one's own experience implies an aspectual rapprochement that is different, yet refers to the same reality in which we develop. Therefore, McLuhan alleged that: "The effects of new media on our sensory lives are similar to the effects of new poetry. They change not our thoughts but the structure of our world."[69] Repeatedly, we see that it is necessary to speak of form in two senses: the first refers to humans and how their accidental form changes due to the media through which they approach reality. The second is a medium's form, determining how humans perceive reality. Thus, Marshall McLuhan insisted that the medium is the message[70] since form determined our knowledge, the content, and the message. This shall be discussed further in the next chapter.

To conclude this chapter on Aristotle's and Marshall McLuhan's theories of formal cause, it may be said that their objectives were different. In one era, Aristotle explored reality as such; therefore, he offered a causal theory that explained the different beings and their behavior. This implies that his four Aristotelian causes allow for intrinsic knowledge of the being. Following this sentiment, it could be argued that the question Aristotle tried to solve with his theory was what is in the nature of the being that moves it to act in a certain way? According to him, the answer, was to be found in each cause but primarily in formal cause, as mentioned earlier. Many lifetimes later, Marshall McLuhan was inspired to explain how a specific being, that is, the human being, acts, although not from an intrinsically motivated point of view. Instead, he focused on the extrinsic causes that move humans to perform any action, either as poiesis or praxis. His research was meant to answer the question: What outside of society moves it to act in a certain way?

This being said, even if each theorist's interest was somewhat different—both aspired to explain humans' actions, despite analyzing different aspects—and they agreed that the way to reach their idiosyncratic goals was via a theoretical framework of the four causes. For Aristotle, the leading cause that gave reason to the actions of beings, in this case, humans, was formal cause

---

69 See: McLuhan Eric, Zingrone Frank. *Essential McLuhan*. Anansi, Toronto 1995, p. 273
70 McLuhan Marshall. *Understanding Media: the Extensions of Man*. MIT Press, London 1994, p. 10

since it is their essence. For him, it was what made them be what they are. In addition, material cause, efficient cause, and final cause can all be reduced to formal cause. For Marshall McLuhan, the explanation regarding humans had to do with formal cause as well, but rather in justifying the idea's importance, albeit his reasons may contradict Aristotle's original theory. In the following chapter, I further develop the theme of form, the medium, as humans' extrinsic cause of action and expand upon the difference of Marshall McLuhan's view of formal cause as compared to Aristotle.

"The Medium is the Message"

In this chapter, I shall explain how Marshall McLuhan saw media in relation to society based on his definition of the medium. According to what he demonstrated, the medium is the most significant factor in the message, beyond the content of the message being communicated. It is how information is contained or transmitted and what determines its influence on the receiver. In addition, I will draw an analogy to Aristotelian theory to better understand the relationship between these two authors regarding each of their conceptions of formal cause.

Humans develop in a reality that is often unknown to them. They act, think, and transform to adjust the environment to themselves. To do so, humans require tools to help them carry out this function in the world. In this context, one might think that the most important factor in this relationship would be that between humans and the world, as they are the two ends seeking to transform each other; albeit one actively and the other passively. Marshall McLuhan identified a third determining element in this relationship, upon which individual and social realities are configured. He called it, "the medium."

McLuhan used his term "medium" to explain rational and social relational structures of humanity. In addition, for him, media were not limited only to the familiar media of communication, as explained above. Instead, much more broadly, McLuhan called any of our extensions a medium[71] because human senses, of which media are extensions, configure our consciousness and experience.[72] As such, our relation to the world is based upon them; they are the intermediary between object and subject. In this view, humans cannot disconnect from media, nor from the impact that they have on them. Instead, "The medium" is the fundamental acting cause of humans, as it shapes and controls the scale and form of human association and action.[73] This is why, notoriously, for Marshall McLuhan, "the medium is the message." Following in his footsteps, we must pay attention to the medium, symbols, and other technologies used, more than content transmitted because the symbolic form

---

71 McLuhan Marshall. *Understanding Media: The Extensions of Man*. MIT Press, London 1994, p. 131
72 *Ibid*, p. 69
73 *Ibid* p. 11

should matter more than the message being sent:

> This revolution involves us willy-nilly in the study of modes and media as forms that shape and reshape our perceptions. That is what I have meant all along by saying the "medium is the message," for the medium determines the modes of perception and the matrix of assumptions within which objectives are set.[74]

Technology, its nature and structure, and not our intentions, are fundamental. The materials with which we work, and the methods we use, are what matter most for the fruit of our labor. We must pay attention to the tools we apply, including the symbols we use to communicate, and other mediators in our social relations, after all these are what move us towards one goal or another.

The phrase, "The medium is the message" implies that different media provide different messages, worldviews and ways of life. This plurality is evident throughout history. In a sense, this was also apparent in Charles Sanders Pierce's (1972) theory of signs, and specifically, when focusing on his distinction between icons and symbols. Expressly, Pierce's pragmatic approach differed from that of dominant hegemonic humanities and scientific theories of his age. Namely, semiotics included a distinct focal difference, abandoning dominant hegemonic norms of the time in favor of a universalizing focus and study of symbols and signs. Procedurally, universalization is also an inevitable part of phonetic alphabetic abstraction. With that said, an understanding based on semiotics is so malleable that any discovered particularity of a sign can be reshaped anew.

As Pierce's semiotics indicated, media of communication are part of our social system. They are seen as reality, containing multiple parts, that may be separated and studied individually to be understood, or universalized, based on symbols and signs in order to understand the whole.[75]

Although, the system we belong to cannot be fully explained by any one of its parts. When one attempts to consequences arise that are often otherwise uncommon. Therefore, this should not be explained as cause and effect. Also, holistically, the more complex and dynamic a system becomes, it becomes more challenging to absolutely explain its effects. Integrally, this illustrates the difficulty in understanding reality through media of communication, since

---

74 McLuhan Eric, Zingrone Frank. *Essential McLuhan*. Anansi, Toronto 1995, p. 188
75 To explain systems theory, I use Lance Strate's paper "Korzybski, Luhmann, and McLuhan" in *Proceedings of the Media Ecology Association*, Vol. 11, 2010 also see Strate, Lance. *On the Binding Biases of Time: And Other Essays on General Semantics and Media Ecology*. New Non-Aristotelian Library Institute of General Semantics, 2011.

these moving targets change and multiply, engendering increasingly complex matrices. It could also be said that complex systems may be understood based on a triangulation of smaller sub-systems. For example, closed social systems like the military, religious affiliations, or educational organizations set a regulatory limit on their membership through enforcement of specific procedures. Other systems are open, enabling interested non-members to join, such as political groups and, nowadays, virtual groups. In truth, each of these systems is distinguished by demarcation lines that, in some cases, are clear, while others are lesser defined. These may be understandable, more or less, depending on one's sense of belonging to the group. Having said that: What is the relationship between these systems and Marshall McLuhan's theories? Communication media function as sub-systems that inform the general system regarding other environments in order to create an internal map of an external reality. We may take, as an example, a person (system) who, through language (sub-system), communicates some information to another person. It seems that according to some authors,[76] the image of the world obtained through this abstraction process is inevitably simplistic and distorted, therefore aspectual.

Marshall McLuhan's stance differed from this approach because, according to him, each technology gradually creates a totally new environment. He saw media not as passive wrappings, but as active processes.[77] This means that whatever is included using language is something new and more profound than what was before. Media of communication do not necessarily bias the

---

76 This was the vision of Niklas Luhmann, a sociologist who specialized in communication theories. He did not see communication as a human action like Jürgen Habermas did, nor as a technological phenomenon or an exchange of information. Humans cannot communicate, *"only communication can communicate."* According to Luhmann, social systems emerge. Communication is produced via *symbolically generalized communication media*, which are different in each social system but comparable to each other due to their structural character. For example, the economic system uses the medium of *money*, the judicial system uses *legal validity*, politics uses *power*, etc. These media determine the systems' codification, reducing their inherent complexity to a binary code: *Payment/Non-Payment, Government/Opposition*, etc. Communication requires a synthesis of three selections: information, utterance, and understanding. Since each one of these components is contingent in itself, it is said that communication becomes improbable in three respects: A) It is improbable that the alter-ego should understand the ego's communication. There is no communication between consciousnesses. B) It is improbable that a communication should reach more persons than are present in the communication. C) It is improbable that a selection according to the expectations of the alter-ego should be accepted and that the ego should take the information as a premise of its own behavior or join further selections. Web. February 22, 2022: https://bit.ly/3v72L91

77 Strate Lance. "Korzybski, Luhmann, and McLuhan" in *Proceedings of the Media Ecology Association*, Vol. 11, 2010, p. 34

information; rather, they produce an interpretation of it, and the possibility of getting to know the environment is contingent upon them. Media may indeed lead us to a better or worse understanding of reality. That is why Marshall McLuhan pointed out the difficulties that they entail, as well as their positive aspects, so that once we know them, we can benefit from this link between systems.

If we analyze this connection, we may notice how human relationships are indirect, both individually and collectively, when considering that each person is a system and is found in the environment. Lance Strate explained this well when he pointed out that stimuli excite and irritate our sense organs and nervous systems, which are our boundary with the environment. It is through our senses that we obtain information from the outer environment; we cannot do it in any other way. Based on this information, we construct an internal map of the environment that surrounds us in a way, more or less, homologous to the outside world. However, this map is not the landscape itself. Therefore, it seems that we live in an inner reality, a conceptual and perceptual environment, and our relationship to the external environment is indirect and mediated by the senses. Thus, Marshall McLuhan reasoned that the medium is the message. This is something that Aristotle also pointed out, albeit differently, of course: There is nothing in the intellect that has not gone through the senses. This shows us, yet again, that mediation exists in human consciousness because our senses are those through which reality is filtered before reaching the intellect. The difference between Aristotle and Marshall McLuhan's perspective on this phenomena is that the former saw the senses as the human being, who's body belonged to them, and who's senses pre-condition them to know reality. There was a clear notion of the human being in Aristotelian philosophy: a being comprised of matter and form. The matter out of which humans are made is indeterminate and underlies change; it is where senses meet. On the other hand, he saw form as the essence of the human being, making human beings what they are, and identifiable by the immaterial soul. Likewise, for Aristotle, form involved the senses because its faculties, or strictly speaking, intelligence, was where sense perceivable data is interpreted. Therefore, according to him, there was a necessary and deep internal human relationship, between matter and form, constituting us.

For Marshall McLuhan, any extension of the human being is a medium,[78] since all that comes from humans is an extension of them, enabling them to relate to the environment. However, if we believe that even humans' senses help them relate to the environment, then the distinction between the medium and

---

78 McLuhan Marshall. *Understanding Media: The Extensions of Man*. MIT Press, London 1994, p. 9

the human being is no longer clear. Following McLuhan's logic, there must be something humans know, as well as a medium through which they go about the process of knowing. However, in Marshall McLuhan's perspective, the knowing boundaries were blurred.

According to Lance Strate, for this reason, the relevant question about "the medium is the message" is, what is the relationship between an internal and external environment? In this regard, Alfred Korzybski[79] asserted in *Science and Sanity* that in order to understand this relationship, one must refer to verbal and semantic environments, as well as to neurolinguistics and neurosemantics. In his own analysis on the subject, he employed the term of "abstracting." Korzybski purposefully used the verb instead of the noun "abstraction" to orient readers away from abstraction as a thing, towards it as a process and activity. Meaningfully, as a verb, "abstract" can be defined in several ways: to summarize, remove, separate, and/or extract. Moreover, the abstracting process takes the external environment into account. Unlike the processes of ingesting and inhaling, abstracting does not involve absorbing any material substance from the environment, Instead, to Korzybski, abstracted information provides an incomplete and selective summary, or map, of the exterior.

Accordingly, all living beings relate in a certain way to their environment; it may be said that in some form, they "engage" with their environment since they respond to certain stimuli for the mere fact of being forms of life. Likewise, organisms with nervous systems communicate via what we call sense perception. Conversely, the human being engages through perception, and in a more complex way, through abstraction, which may be called symbolic communication and is carried out through language and other systems of symbols that help humans generate and accumulate knowledge.

---

79 "How is it that humans have progressed so rapidly in science, mathematics, and engineering, yet we continue to exhibit behaviors that result in misunderstanding, suspicion, bigotry, hatred, and even violence in our dealings with other people and with other cultures?" Alfred Korzybski pursued this question as an engineer, military officer, and extraordinary observer of human behavior. He survived the horrific battlegrounds of World War I and wondered why humans could progress and advance in some areas but not in others. He theorized that the attitudes and methodologies responsible for advancements in engineering, the sciences, and mathematics could be applied to the daily affairs of individuals, and ultimately cultures. Web. May 15, 2013, http://www.generalsemantics.org/the-general-semantics-learning-center/alfred-korzybski/. He called this new field "general semantics" and introduced it as a practical and teachable system in his 1933 book, *Science and Sanity*. He died in 1950, just as his theory was beginning to have greater relevance to other fields, including cybernetics. Marshall McLuhan was in touch with individuals close to general semantics, and spoke about systems in his work *Understanding Media: The Extensions of Man*, MIT Press, London 1994. Therefore, Korzybski is considered relevant to this theme.

According to Korzybski's vision, one could point out that although it is true that every of form of life on earth has a way of developing in the environment, each one does so through mediation, but in a different way, subject to the type of being in question. For example, one could argue that plants do not have knowledge, as such, of reality, but rather their "engagement" with the environment has to do with their biological needs, their natural instincts lead them to nurture themselves, grow, and regenerate unconditionally. Said otherwise, no abstraction of the environment is being done by the plant. Nevertheless, in another sense plants do communicate with their environments when moving their roots instinctively toward, in search of, water. And when they carry out photosynthesis from being affected by the sun. Therefore, we can say that there is a unique and very rudimentary symbolic system of communication through which plant life forms relate to the environment. On a related vein, in the case of animals, there are more complex relationships compared to that of simpler beings. Animals are capable of knowing their environment via their senses, and even modifying them, in order to survive. For instance, a bird can build its nest against the laws of nature, since twigs do not naturally lump together to form nests. And, in addition, the bird knows to build the nest in high places in order to protect its hatchlings. Bees, which are excellent builders of honeycombs, are another example. In fact, Karl Marx concluded that, in this sense, this kind of insect could be compared to the best human architects, perhaps even surpassing them, since their natural instincts prompt them to protect their species. Bees appear to know the actions needed, as well as the elements they necessary to sustain their lives adequately. Nevertheless, and as Marx also indicated, despite seeming perfection among animals, bees do have a fault; they are incapable of building anything that is not a honeycomb. Similarly, birds also cannot build anything different from their nests, since each of their actions is pre-determined by their nature and the continuity of their species. This is not the case in humans.

This behavior of animals demonstrates that they also "engage" with the environment, know their medium, and learn from it, and from their predecessors, how to survive. They know what surrounds them and have learned from their experiences. Unlike plants, animals have senses that allow them to access certain features of reality that not even humans are able to as readily. Bats, for example, are blind and possess the sonar sense, echolocation, perceiving the closeness or distance of something based on its vibration. By their nature, humans are incapable of doing this.

Furthermore, in regards to the relationship between animals and the environment, some philosophers have argued that animals do have their own "languages" which they use to communicate among their own species. One would need then to expand the definition of language to understand its limits. If we see language as a system of symbols used in order to communicate, then animals definitively have language, and even plants do, since in practice, anything can be considered a symbol; a flower that blossoms, the moment a flower wilts, and so forth. In the case of animals, it is more evident. They are capable of making sounds that indicate specific things to their species and even to others. We are able to understand that when a dog barks, it may be angry, scared, etc., meaning that there are sounds the animal makes that "communicate" its circumstances.

Following this line of thought, one could consider another definition of language as a method of communication established to express ideas, emotions, and wishes through a system of deliberately transmitted symbols. This definition would formulate language as an exclusively human method because, as far as we know, only humans are capable of expressing ideas, emotions, and wishes based on words, drawings, gestures, and abstracting languages. In addition, that we know of, humans are the only beings on earth capable of choosing symbols for communication. Globally, and in different dialects, we show that we can through Spanish, English, gestures, etc.

To make myself clear, the theme of language is crucial for this study because, as I will demonstrate in a more detailed discussion below, methods of communication transmit ideas, emotions, and wishes, and their varying mediations modify the way a person receives a message.

Irrespective of which definition of language we choose to use, it could be said that how humans and animals communicate differs greatly. Human language is not as instinctive as we perceive it to be in animals. Human beings have a convention in symbols that appears to be undoable by other beings, which are more oriented through the world by their biology. The number of messages animals transmit is limited. Whereas we formulate ideas in categorical ways and are able to grow our symbolic repertoires. As far as we know, this is not the case for other beings. Thinking back to Korzybski's insistence that living beings relate symbolically or via abstraction, one could conclude that this engagement or relationship with environments is uniquely human, as only humanity is capable of recognizing it as such, willfully interacting in a variety of choice ways.

Other language scholars have also dealt with this relationship with the environment. A representative case being Susanne Langer[80] who noted that perception was a symbolic activity, a form of metonymy with which we take a fraction of the environment, highlighting a part of the whole. Along similar

---

80   Susanne Katherina Langer (1895-1985), was an American whose main interests were philosophy of mind and aesthetics and was influenced by Ernst Cassirer and Alfred North Whitehead.

lines, Marshall McLuhan argued that language was a form of perception, and he so far as to describe languages as human organs of perception. For both, perception and language contributed to the maintenance and functional limits of self-organizing social systems.

As I have demonstrated throughout this study, abstraction accompanies that of symbolic communication since the process requires that we take something from reality in order to then communicate or inform others through the use of language. In his own work, Lance Strate has also contributed to literature, further unpacking and generating understanding, regarding the process of abstracting.[81] For him, "abstracting" is associated with technological activity, since based on what we take from the environment, we get to know our world and determine certain needs to satisfy based on technology. One example being, when humans perceived an inadequate climate for survival, they built houses to live in. Another would be that when humans perceived the need to move from one place to another rapidly, they first built wheels, then carts, and then, finally, cars.

Relatedly, Marshall McLuhan used the term "technology" synonymously with the word "medium" because he saw all inventions and innovations as media through which we relate to the environment. Typically, technology is seen as standing in opposition to biology because it is artificial rather than natural. But, as detailed thus far, McLuhan in his work *Understanding Media* explained that our being is extended through technologies. The latter mediate between the body and the environment. These meidations are also present in the animal world; chimpanzees use sticks to eat ants and birds use twigs to build their nests. Therefore, it seems technology is part of our nature. It is intrinsic to the survival of the species. Technological artifacts can potentially be used in a variety of ways, but the material features of any one tool affords the user a range of possibilities for said use. On the flip side, one cannot use a spoon to slice or a coffee maker to write. Functional limitations aside, we should consider whether certain instances of technological use may contradict the purpose of a technology. Asked otherwise, if a computer were to be used as a door stopper, would that contribute to computer technology? Or if one threw a piano through a window, would that constitute musical technology? And, if a book was given to someone illiterate, or to someone unable to read a specific language in which it was written, is that technology being used? It seems that when a technological tool is used in a different way from which

---

81   See: Strate, Lance. "Korzybski, Luhmann, and McLuhan" in *Proceedings of the Media Ecology Association*, Vol. 11, 2010, p. 36 and Strate Lance. *On the Binding Biases of Time: And Other Essays on General Semantics and Media Ecology*. New Non-Aristotelian Library Institute of General Semantics, 2011.

it was intended, this process may be considered a *reinvention*. As in, through alternative use of an object, it is transformed into something essentially new.[82] This would imply that an object is determined through utilization, which is definitively possible today, most of all because we have a concept that illustrates this modification in objects. What would Aristotle think of this matter? As discussed previously, for him, the being of things, both natural and artificial, was determined by form. In that case, what might Aristotle believe happens to objects used out of accordance with their essence? Perhaps he would argue that, realistically, there is no reinvention. But, that the object is merely forced into an unnatural direction, and that if this its force were extreme enough, the being would transform into something totally different; that is, its form, its essence would change, as well as its purpose. In some sense, maybe artificial objects are "reinvented" more easily since humans are the ones who determine their definitions. In comparison, the definition of natural things is less clear. As much as humans may wish a tree was not a tree, unless they forcibly intervene, the tree will not stop being a tree. On the contrary, artificial things differ. Consider the previous discussion of televisions, intended to project content. If humans decided that from now on TVs are for holding doors open, that is their new role, and resultingly they will cease to project.

As we can see, the application is an intrinsic element of the technology itself. We cannot talk of objects without their use, even when thinking about paintings or sculptures, which are used passively, for example, as decoration. The above illustrated what the application of one thing or another can be. The feature of a tool points in a certain direction towards its regular application. This is what Marshall McLuhan referred to when he said that the medium is the message. For example, electric light can be used to read, illuminate streets or offices at night, to spell on letters or signs, project movies, examine teeth at the dentist's office, or simply as a decoration. Nevertheless, each of these uses pales in comparison to the impact electric light has alone as a medium and a technology, significantly altering our way of life, including how we work and play, how we decorate, and how we conduct ourselves in the world in general. Also, the introduction of electric light eliminated some difference between day and night. When electric light was introduced, it revolutionized our ability to work day and night, in whatever space, and provided an option to choose naturally darkness or an illuminated surroundings. In ancient times this was inconceivable. Then, the best time for humans to be active was during natural light because it enabled better vision for labor. Today, due to light this limitation has been eclipsed, transforming society dramatically. Next, I further expand on

---

82 Strate, Lance. "If It´s Neutral, It´s Not Technology", *Educational Technology*/January-February 2012, p. 6-9

this subject by analyzing media of communication.

Keep in mind that when Marshall McLuhan insisted that media altered our central nervous systems, there was no contemporaneous scientific evidence to support that. In the meantime, ample evidence has been documented that reading books, using computer, and other mediums, regardless of the content, each uniquely affect our brain function. This work illustrates how media affect us not simply through messaging alone, but also via the form they are presented. Fundamentally, humans are controlled by technology; it is true that we can change a TV channel if/when we do not like a program. W can also turn the TV off at will, implying that we are able to measure the effects of the medium. But could we choose to live in a world without television? Individually, we may decide never to board a ship or train, but our choice alone does not remove the effects of said mediums on society. We do not have the freedom to opt for a world without bombs or guns. We can support disarmament, argue against these media, but not free ourselves from their impacts.

Therefore, we can contend that we exist in a dynamic relationship with technologies that feed and alter us. Even so, we do not command, nor lack complete control over, these extensions of ourselves. Rather, they could be said to move in the space found in-between.[83]

> It's always been the artist (...) who recognizes that the future is the present, and uses his work to prepare the ground for it. But most people (...) are ignorant of what the media do to them; unaware that because of their pervasive effects on man, it is the medium itself that is the message, not the content, and unaware that the medium is also the message.[84]

On the other hand, the technologies we develop help us abstract information from our environment. They allow us to gather, share, retain knowledge, and communicate and join others in novel ways. Additionally, they enable us to transform our environment(s) and function within them. Swiss playwrite and novelist, Max Frisch noted this in *Homo Faber* when he said, "technology is the art of never having to experience the world."[85] Media help us develop in the environment, but also condition our relationship with it. As explained above, they highlight an aspect of reality, which implies a disregard of the rest. For Marshall McLuhan, media and technology were extensions of the human

---

83 See: Strate Lance. "If It's Neutral, It's Not Technology", *Educational Technology*/January-February 2012, p. 6-8 and Strate, Lance. Media Ecology: An Approach to Understanding the Human Condition. P. Lang, 2017.
84 McLuhan Eric, Zingrone Frank. *Essential McLuhan*. Anansi, Toronto 1995, p. 237
85 Frisch Max. *Homo Faber: A report*. Harcourt, San Diego 1959, p. 178

organism, and our media numbed our bodies and minds. As overviewed, to him, each extension was an amputation since the extending medium is located between us and the world, serving as a barrier between both. These barriers become part of our space and of the boundaries separating the system (our system) from reality. This theme was expanded upon in the first chapter.

Every time we know something, we filter information, we mediate, or as Strate puts it, the medium is the system's membrane. And, in turn, that membrane is us. Connectedly, whatever is in the system, the content, is us, and the boundaries that mediate reality are the membrane that, in turn, separate us from the "other."

Therefore, the phrase *the medium is the message* implies that we must begin at the center, with the medium. The medium comes first. Before the sculpture, we have stone and chisel. Before the painting, we have paint, color, brushes. With language, the newborn first cries and screams, then begins to babble, and from there, language emerges, those first words with which it will attain true human communication. Before being able to form any words, we must listen to the sounds around us to learn and imitate them. Following this process, the medium can be the content of another medium. Thus, discourse is the content of the writing, the writing is the content of the print, and so forth. Once the medium becomes content, it is reduced to an element of style, and loses its importance as a shaper of content. Consequently, one can say: "media in all things, including media."[86] Logically speaking, this was likely why Marshall McLuhan began with communication media, eventually expanding his concept of the medium to include all technology.

For these reasons, we can make a comparison to Aristotelian philosophy in this sense: From an Aristotelian point of view, it would be difficult to talk about something that "mediates" between humans and reality since, for him, humans were a compound of matter and form. As such, Aristotle believed that human beings have certain functions that depend on the whole and cannot be separated. This also includes the case of knowledge, which is mediated via senses (matter), and intelligence (matter), and have more to do with form, or with the essence, of a being in question.

On the other hand, for Marshall McLuhan, beings of any kind were not divided into multiple parts either. However, he aimed to explain what determined human knowledge in more detail, hence his desire to distinguish between a medium and what it contained. Now that this has been clarified, we may say that for Aristotle too, what mediated between humans and their world were the senses. This is because senses allow us to perceive our own

---

86 See: Strate L., Wachtel E. "Media Transcendence", *The Legacy of McLuhan*. Hampton Press, Inc. New Jersey, 2005, p. 29

aspectual realities. However, senses do not act on their own. They are not totally independent; they are the conditions that make our knowledge gathering possible. Both Aristotle and Marshall McLuhan would agree. As discussed, as far as we know, sensory perception differs between animals and humans. And yet, other beings can obtain specific and concrete knowledge of things. In other words, a being's own essence could be said to limit their capacity to obtain certain knowledges. Meaning, for humans, their form or essence determines only so many possibilities of generating their conceptions of knowledge. Due to form, abstraction of reality itself occurs, and humans can only know reality based on its causes. They can know that a chair's material cause is wood, as well as its formal cause, to learn that "it is a chair," defining it as such. They can also say it was made by a carpenter, and lastly, they can enunciate its purpose, which is to provide a seat. This deliberation implies that humans have a more profound knowledge of things, determined by their rational form. Thus, we may conclude that what determines knowledge, in Aristotelian terms, is form. And, furthermore, that it contains matter since we could not speak of human form, or anything else, without it. Analogous to this, we can say that the medium is form and the message is matter, or as McLuhan said: "The effect of media, like their message, is really in their form and not in their content."[87]

These levels of abstraction can also be analyzed from the point of view of the media that provide us with knowledge. For instance, one might refer to this in terms of form and matter, or as McLuhan pointed out, of a medium and a message, from which we perceive certain things that modify our being. For Korzybski, sense perception constituted the lowest level of abstraction, symbolizing a higher level. In his view, images were less abstract than words; therefore, animals had a lesser knowledge than humans. According to Korzybski, animals therefore could not separate themselves from their senses in order to gain knowledge. On the flip side, there is evidence that humans can because when reality passes through our senses, it arrives at intelligence, enabling human capacity to deduce or induce information, obsolescing the need to refer back to reality at any given moment. If and when, animals do gain knowledge via images, they need a mental picture or the species' image to be able to know their environment. Whereas, for humans, while images remain important, they can do without them, instead learning through use of words or other signs.

When we think about media of communication, television is less abstract than a book, and the written word is more abstract than the spoken word.

---

[87] McLuhan Marshall. "Myth and the Mass Media". *Daedalus* Vol. 88, No. 2, 1959, MIT Press, p. 339-342

This is why, according to Walter Ong,[88] writing was a secondary symbol system representing speech, our primary symbol system, in a sense that writing consisted of symbols which represent other symbols.[89] Marshall McLuhan also acknowledged this fact, but added that there are qualitative distinctions of any one media type. For him, television and cinema are different medias; therefore, as Lance Strate explains, they represent different methods of abstracting. One is not necesarily more or less abstract than any other; they are just qualitatively different. The same could be said of other medias of communication, such as radio, newspapers, papyrus, parchment, hieroglyphs, and/or dialogue. Also, scholars, like Strate have since associated this with linguistic relativism,[90] arguing that any one language orients different modes of abstraction and mediation. This will be analyzed in the following chapter.

Perceptual forms also represent different modes of abstraction. For instance, sense of sight is different than to hearing, touch, smell, or taste. This is why, literate people abstract differently than nonliterates. This calls for an analysis of modes of knowledge, as well as how humans perceive everyday realities, focusing on media and form, since "the medium is the message." With this core idea in mind, Marshall McLuhan called took an interdisciplinary approach including communicology, linguistics, history, and philosophy, attending to the medium rather than content. He did so despite the norm of ignoring media to focus on content. According to Lance Strate, a prominent media ecologist, McLuhan's aim was for the human mind and spirit to be self-liberated from subjugation inflicted by our own symbol systems and other technologies.[91] For McLuhan, this could only happen with attention toward mediums because they impact our development, mediating between us and realities. The medium, and not the message, is what is sent or received because as belabored, media determine what can be known from the message and/or the perception to be gained from it. Symbolic form is what is most significant, which McLuhan detailed as such:

---

88   Walter J. Ong (1912 – 2003), An American English, French, and Psychology professor, renowned rhetorician and theologian. Explored the transformation caused in human consciousness when oral cultures become cryptographic. He identified a "secondary orality" that arose in Western societies with the arrival of the telephone, the television, and new electronic technologies.

89   See: Strate Lance. "Korzybski, Luhmann, and McLuhan" in *Proceedings of the Media Ecology Association*, Vol. 11, 2010, p. 31-42 and Strate, Lance. *On the Binding Biases of Time: And Other Essays on General Semantics and Media Ecology*. New Non-Aristotelian Library Institute of General Semantics, 2011, p. 19

90   Edward Sapir (1921), Benjamin Lee Whorf (1956) and Dorothy Lee (1959) in Strate Lance, "Korzybski, Luhmann, and McLuhan" in *Proceedings of the Media Ecology Association*, Vol. 11, 2010, p. 31-42

91   See: Strate A. Lance. "Studying Media as Media: McLuhan and the Media Ecology Approach", *Media Tropes eJournal*, Vol. 1 (2008) p. 130

> The mass media are extensions of the mechanisms of human perception; they are imitators of the modes of human apprehension and judgment.[92]

With that said, technological structure, not intent, is what affects humans. The materials being shaped and methods employed are what predominantly impact the outcome of all actions.

However, some people disagree with this position. For example, and as Strate indicates, the United States National Rifle Association (NRA) insists there is no problem with possessing guns, claiming that there is no need for gun control because "guns don't kill people, people do." Many may agree with this slogan, including some philosophers, like Thomas Aquinas himself. For example, in his work he attested that anything created by God is good.[93] In his logic, guns are God's creation, being that they originated from natural elements, making them what they are. Cast this way, guns are not evil so much as they are tools for human action, enabling self-defense and/or survival skills. In this light, evil resides in humans since they are the ones who use creations in the wrong way, for purposes that are opposed to nature. For Strate, those who disagree with this argument and believe that there is more potential for violence with guns, than without them, agree that the medium is the message. To him, in great measure, what determines human action is the medium, not the content or form, and not matter. On the other hand, there is no need to reduce technology and media's value to the level of binaries, like good or evil, harmful or beneficial, functional or dysfunctional. Instead, we can analyze the different channels afforded by technology from quantitative and qualitative points of view, just as Marshall McLuhan himself probed. Therefore, when we think about a stone we find on the ground, we might observe its physical characteristics, distinguishing the object from other elements in the area, by detailing its weight, density, and matter. Yet, on the ground a stone is likely not to be seen as technology, as much as a neutral object. But the moment it is picked up from the ground and thrown, it is transformed into a form of technology, or extension, of the thrower's being intended to reach a certain distance.

Expanding on this idea, the medium is the message because content cannot

---

92 Carpenter E. and McLuhan Marshall. eds., *Explorations in Communication: An Anthology* (Boston: Beacon Press, 1960), 180, http://www.questia.com/read/91604761.
93 Being, as such, has not the aspect of repugnance but only of fittingness; because being is common to all things. But being, inasmuch as it is this determinate being, has an aspect of repugnance to some determinate being. And in this way, one being is hateful to another, and is evil; though not in itself, but by comparison with something else. Web. https://www.newadvent.org/summa/2029.htm

exist without a medium.⁹⁴ As in, how could we make something known if not through a way, or channel, that carried or contained information? Thus, we could say that the medium is form since the latter "contains" information that a medium needs in order to "be." Just as matter needs form, so content needs matter. To pose an analogy, form for Aristotle was crucial for content, even though the reference he made in this sense was to matter because, as outlined by him, matter (content) needed form (medium) to "be." Just as a message needs to be transmitted from a vessel, matter needs form to transmit its information. Let us illustrate this further by means of some examples: when thinking about mind and body, we could consider the body as a medium from which the mind comes. The mind is not the body, but it emerges from it, is contained in it, depends on it, but can also affect and alter it. From a different point of view, according to Strate, the body's content is another medium. Physiologically, cells are in our bloodstream. Equally, technology is the content, and biology is the medium since biology produces, extends, and also acts in/of it. To date, various experiments have taken place, mainly concerning the function of the brain and its relationship with technology. Devices have been inserted in the brain testing how foreign mechanical parts behave as part of the whole.

Another example is implantation of electrodes in the brain of a person with Parkinson's disease, for purposes of balancing the signals sent to the brain. By conducting these experiments, it has also been found that these signals can produce movements in those without any ailments[95].

Technology, as a medium, can also change and use biology as content. The conscious brain can be seen as the message, and the unconscious brain as the medium. This coincides with Jung's (1968) theory regarding the psyche, or prior to that that, Saint Augustine (1961) who, in work on the matter presented time as a medium that contains the past and the future. Specifically, his idea was that the soul was the medium that contained the present, past, and future because without it we would be incapable of perceiving each one of these theoretical periods as demarcations in time.

With these temporal distinctions laid on the table, one could argue that chaos is the medium that contains order because, in accordance with theories of evolution, order stems from disorder.

Finally, and as Strate delineates in his own research, evil is only the content that many times monopolizes our attention, whereas good is the medium that

---

94   See: Strate A. Lance. "Studying Media as Media: McLuhan and the Media Ecology Approach", *Media Tropes eJournal*, Vol. 1 (2008) p. 127-142

95   See: *Implanting stimulating electrodes in patient´s brain,* courtesy of Hagai Berman from Hebrew University. Web. June 29, 2013 https://class.coursera.org/bluebrain-001/lecture/index

constitutes our invisible environment.[96] That being the case, according to him, we should not lose sight of the medium. The medium is the foremost element in the relationship between the individual and the environment, and, ultimately, the one that contains and carries the information perceived in and from reality.

According to Marshall McLuhan, form, the medium, effectively determined content. This could also be seen in communication; words could take the form of speech or writing, they were their medium, or they ccould exist internally in the mind, be contained in them. In his eyes, words could not exist by themselves; they needed a medium to contain and carry them. In addition, the various forms via which words are transmitted determined what they signify and the impact they had. For Strate, the words that we think look different when we express them. We cannot always express our thoughts and feelings in words. Also, the words we use are everlasting, they exist at a distance from whoever uttered them considering they can be read and interpreted by another, and finally, they have an impersonal quality compared to speech. We shall delve further into the subject of the alphabet and orality to underline their importance as the media of the transmitted message.

Information always has a form: chemical sequences, on paper, in codes, etc., determining not only their qualities but also the access of certain people who can decipher this code. If the medium changes, so does the information. For Marshall McLuhan, the medium is the message because the content of a medium is to a certain extent another medium. This leads to the question: Then, where is information? Or rather: What is information? If, to him, the medium contained another medium, and so on, ad infinitum, we could say that there are only "forms," "media" without content. So, what is actually being transmitted? On another hand, to McLuhan, the word already contained a message with its own meaning. The message is already contained in the form. However, an experience is required to be able to understand a message's form. No message is universal; it is rather created by each speaker to communicate and transform their environment. Also, there is content within each human being, a message to be expressed through different media. The problem arises in distinguishing a message from its medium that carries it since it becomes part of it as it is transmitted. That is why Marshall McLuhan explained that the medium of speech becomes the content of writing, that the medium of writing became the content of print, the medium of print became the content of hypertext,[97] and so onward with each new media type.

---

96 Strate L., Wachtel E. "Media Transcendence", *The Legacy of McLuhan*. Hampton Press, Inc. New Jersey, 2005, p. 31

97 See: Strate A. Lance. "Studying Media as Media: McLuhan and the Media Ecology Approach", *Media Tropes eJournal*, Vol. 1 (2008), p. 131

The *McLuhanistic*[98] position regarding media has been subject of multiple criticisms, mainly regarding his expression "The Medium is the message." Some critics indicate that the medium is *not* the message, to the point that this expression has become a cliché.[99] Some of his critics see this phrase as a mathematical equation to be understood literally, but this is not the case. There is a lack of understanding of Marshall McLuhan's theory since this expression is a metaphor. Others have retorted that the phrase is a contradiction, and an oxymoron,[100] that uses two significant oppositional concepts in the same expression, creating a third concept. Given that the literal meaning of an oxymoron is the opposite to point of absurdity, the reader or interlocutor is expected to understand this expression metaphorically. Upon deper examination, this criticism does not seem correct because McLuhan regularly used expressions that should not be taken literally, as a personal style. McLuhan's idiosyncrasies should be made clear to readers, otherwise they are bound to misunderstand the purpose of his approach. In addition, judging expressions out of context is poor practice, as it may lead to an interpretation entirely opposition to authorial intent.

Other critics have admonished that due to Marshall McLuhan's emphasis on the medium, he completely lost the content. As detiled in previous sections, it should be noted that it would not be possible to talk about a medium without content; a claim McLuhan attempted is to make central, despite the content dominant paradigm of the age. Notably, the messages being sent may be the same, even repeated over lifetimes, but it is the tools used to transmit them which have changed our way of acting, thinking, and being. Today's humans are not the same as they were 2000 years ago. Our society, communities, and language have all changed, but what we are saying continues, in essence, to be the same. The message is the foundation of communication, but the tool is what distinguishes it from others. This last critique highlights the paramount role of the message in communication. At the end of the day, the message is what motivates usage of a medium. However, we should remember that technology is what shapes us, both as individuals and collectively.

Some critics have referred to Marshall McLuhan as a technological determinist who negated humans' free will within his documentations of how technologies shape our orientations:

---

98   A term coined in France thanks to the unprecedented success of Marshall McLuhan's theory regarding media of communication.
99   See: Strate A. Lance. "Studying Media as Media: McLuhan and the Media Ecology Approach", *Media Tropes eJournal*, Vol. 1 (2008), p. 132
100   Gozzi Ray. *The power of metaphor in the age of electronic media*. Hampton Press, New Jersey 1999

> The message of any medium or technology is the change of scale or pace or pattern that it introduces into human affairs. The railway did not introduce movement or transportation or wheel or road into human society, but it accelerated and enlarged the scale of previous human functions, creating totally new kinds of cities and new kinds of work and leisure. This happened whether the railway functioned in a tropical or northern environment and is quite independent of the freight or content of the railway medium.[101]

Following McLuhan's doctrine, we are involuntarily shaped by tools and are incapable of refusing or conceding such change since, in effect, we are not conscious of the influence of the environment. In this way, the media, are our essence. As McLuhan insisted, the problem is that attention has narrowed to the information orienting a mass loss of sight regarding what matters: the medium. However, according to Strate, Marshall McLuhan never used the term "determinism" nor said anything against human action. In *The Medium is the Message*, McLuhan refuted this critique by merely clarifying: "There is absolutely no inevitability as long as there is a willingness to contemplate what is happening."[102] Also, he reminded that freedom does not imply a lack of boundaries or external influences. In his book *Diffusion of Innovations*, researcher Everett Rogers[103] indicated that innovation had consequences, for better and worse. Many of them stemming from the introduction of new technologies—and the not always desirable consequences—that do manifest indirect effects of each new medium or technology. This implies that the reality we live in is the result of our wishes. But, on the other hand, this also causes certain unintended consequences, that continue to socially and materially transform our realities.

Others have highlighted favorable aspects of Marshall McLuhan's theories of media. Bruce Powers,[104] who was a very close collaborator of McLuhan, defended that Marshall's research should not be considered a technique so much as a position, approach, or unrelenting analysis. Powers argued that

---

101 McLuhan Marshall. *Understanding Media: the extensions of man*. MIT Press, London 1994, p. 8
102 McLuhan M. and FIORE Q. *The Medium is the Massage: An Inventory of effects*. Ginko Press, California 1967
103 Everett M. Rogers was a communication theorist and sociologist best known for his theory on innovation and for introducing the term *early adopter*.
104 A collaborator of Marshall McLuhan, with whom he published *The Global Village* in which they suggested that today's users of technology are caught between two very different ways of perceiving the world.

many times McLuhan's work led to "semantic wedges,"[105] such as the very well-known expression, "The medium is the message." If one subscribes to this understanding of his work, the popular phrase can be seen as not purporting a literal description of what occurs with media, but rather a call to action for media consumers to take notice of the medium and not the content. In addition, Arthur Kroker indicates that Marshall McLuhan was a technological humanist interested in sending a "shock wave"[106] to his readers on their journey towards the new digital era.

McLuhan was interested in using language to spark a series of hypotheses about electronic media surrounding humans. Guided by this purpose, he used aphorisms, jokes, grandiloquence, ironic counterpoints, paradoxes, and "thematic counterpoint" to demystify the printed page and recreate the "technological massage" experience. For example, this particular expression metaphorically indicated how technology impacted humans, how the environment changed human attitude and movement, their inescapable influences, interwoven so pervasively within our world, they go unnoticed. According to Kroker, Marshall McLuhan's work comprised a technological discourse, significantly examining social life and technological dependency. As such, he stressed: "McLuhan was the last and best exponent of the liberal imagination in Canadian letters."[107] No matter if as a critic or supporter, all aforementioned theorists agreed that McLuhan made enormous impact thanks to his unorthodox approach to media, documenting their influence on our relations.

Marshall McLuhan's research was not limited to mere observation and/ or recitation of facts, prophesizing our current reality. He sought to change the influence of media and transform its negative invisibility into something

---

105   See: Powers Bruce. "Final thoughts: A collaborator on Marshall's methods and meanings", *Journal of Communication 31*, 1981, p. 189-190

106   Arthur Kroker is the University of Victoria Canada research Chair in Technology, Culture, and Theory, Professor of Political Science and Director of the Pacific Center for Technology and Culture (PACTAC) at the university. Together with Marilouise Kroker, he is the editor of the internationally acclaimed peer-reviewed *journal Theory and Critical Digital Studies: A Reader* (University of Toronto Press). His more recent publications are *The Will to Technology and the Culture of Nihilism: Heidegger, Nietzsche, and Marx* (University of Toronto Press) and *Born-Again Ideology: Religion, Technology and Terrorism*. In addition to a translation into Japanese of *The Will to Technology*, eleven of Dr. Kroker's books have been published in German, Italian, Japanese, and Croatian. His current research focuses on the new field of critical digital studies and the politics of the body in contemporary techno-culture. See: Kroker Arthur. *Technology and the Canadian Mind*. New World Perspectives, Montreal, 1984, p. 14

107   Kroker Arthur. *Technology and the Canadian mind*. New World Perspectives, Montreal, 1984, p. 78

positive for humanity. This is why he proposed paying attention to the medium and considering its importance on individual lives and larger society. It is said, he found inspiration in Edgar Allan Poe's short story "A Descent into the Maelstrom," a tale of a sailor who fell into the water and was caught in a whirlpool, narrowly escaping death to find a hidden pattern in the vortex. These maelstroms could be compared to our media, in that the only way to escape them, avoiding their unconscious human configurations, are through analysis and recognition of their moving patterns. This would not be possible through linear or direct analysis, but rather, dialectic research for purposes of revealing the processes and media effects on our lives.

Every medium gives its content certain characteristics that change its significance. In the following chapter, I analyze some communication channels, which consist of forms that change individuals, and thus, society, highlighting the medium over the message in a McLuhanesque style.

Media's Qualities as the Individual's and Society's Formal Cause

> "...the *beholding* of *idols*, or the *use of technology*, conforms men to *them*."
>
> —Marshall McLuhan

Thus far we have overviewed both Aristotle's and Marshall McLuhan's concepts of formal cause to better understand their theories and adequately interpret each of their claims. We also illustrated how the concept of formal cause relate to media of communication, as this is key to understanding McLuhan's expression, "the medium is the message." This chapter will focus on the importance of this theory concerning society and reality, since "the media," as Marshall McLuhan called them, produce effects in those who receive their content, not so much due to the information they convey, but rather to the qualities of each of these channels of communication.

To demonstrate this perspective, within this chapter I frame several media of communication as formal causes of individuals and society, in order to show how various media impact human reasoning differently, including the favorable and adverse effects each one may invoke.

It has since been alleged that Marshall McLuhan's theory regarding mass media, as elements that conditioned and disseminated messages and images, was revolutionary. In fitting with his proposition that, "the medium is the message," As repeated, McLuhan maintained that mass media exercised a strong influence on humans and society regarding form. A last example being, writer and artist Richard Kostelanetz who said, "the most extraordinary quality of McLuhan's mind is that it discerns significance where others see only data or nothing; he tells us how to measure phenomena previously unmeasurable."[108]

As overviewed previously, Marshall McLuhan's analysis did not apply only

---

108   Web. May 28, 2013 http://www.nytimes.com/books/97/11/02/home/mcluhan-magazine.html

to mass media. His definition of media included any technology that created an extension of the human body and senses, from clothing to the computer. In his interview with the Salvat publishing house, he said:

> Considering that societies have always been more conditioned by the nature of their mass media than by the message these transmit, we must conclude, then, that whenever a new technology penetrates a society, it saturates all of its institutions. Technology is a revolutionary agent; we prove that today with electronic media and the same occurred centuries ago with the invention of the phonetic alphabet.[109]

According to him, all media served as active metaphors in their power to translate experiences into new form.[110] He emphasized that how information reached the individual depended upon the medium, which "determined," in some way, the message being expressed. To McLuhan, this limitation led the message receiver to receive the information in a "particular" way, given that the message (matter), is configured by the medium (the form) through which a message is transmitted. His perspective implied that the information that arrived from a sender was partial because biases of a channel alter a message, in turn, influencing a receivers interpretation of it. To him, this happened because the individual who received a message each embody their own form, which also determined their thinking, perceiving, or experience of phenomena in different ways.

In a basic sense, one might say that in any information sequence is theoretically comprised of: a) the message, b) the medium, and c) the individuals sending and/or receiving information. Here, at least two forms could be said to determine two different matters. In this dynamic, b) the medium would be the form or channel that contains information to be transmitted. According to any one medium's formal qualities, certain aspects of the information sent through it will be highlighted. For example, if one were to emphasize a) a message supporting family values, one could do so in several ways; writing an article or presenting a speech, for a few examples. In the case of the former, the author might emphasize reasons as to why humans should live as families, leaving some reader's questions unanswered. In the medium of an article, any one reader would select and interpret the written information according to their own lived experiences; thus, not all of the important information will necessarily reach

---

109 McLuhan Marshall. "Teoría de la imagen", *Salvat*. Salvat Editores, Barcelona 1973, p. 8-23 (in Spanish)

110 McLuhan Marshall. *Understanding Media: The Extensions of Man*. MIT Press, London 1994, p. 124

the receiver, regardless of author intention. On the other hand, a speech might be understandable to those who speak the presenter's language, and could therefore be described as more accessible compared to written mediums, only accessible to literate people, and/or those able to have the article be read to them by someone else able to read. In addition, as a medium, in person speeches require physical co-presence of speaker and audience, allowing the audience to interact with the speaker. Presenters are presumably experts in a given field, trained to more effectively transmit messages on a topic than laypeople. Here, what matters is not only a speaker's views, but also those of the public, that are present receivers of information.

The above discussion traced out a few examples of how different aspects of the same information can be made known differently, based on the medium used to portray a message.

Additionally, c) the forms of any one individual sending and/or receiving information also determine the ways in which information is received. As discussed in the first chapter, human form is comprised of certain accidental aspects that make an individual the person they "are." These accidents of essence distinguish individuals from others. In other words, an individual's form shapes how another individual might receive information from them, especially those most subjected to discriminatory paradigms or prejudices. With that said, analyzing form as an individual determinant lies outside the scope of this project, entailing a review of each individual, era, and culture, etc., to gain a comprehensive look. This would be practically impossible. Therefore, I limit the present study to specifically form, the media which transmit information.

Speech as Formal Cause
Words and Essence

One of the first and most important media in human development is speech. It is the ideal medium, as it allows humans to relate to other individuals of their own species. For Marshall McLuhan, the spoken word was the first technology by which humans were able to let go of their environment in order to grasp it in a new way.[111] Speech bonds the intellect and the world, and through it, we can call or name what is around us. Through speech, humans create a closer relationship with the world, recognizing it as something foreign and external to them, but also as part of their reality because the world is where they exist and develop.

---

111 McLuhan Marshall. *Understanding Media: The Extensions of Man*. MIT Press, London 1994, p. 69

Humans are the only beings we are aware of on earth capable of perceiving reality and giving it a name through the use of words. This phenomenon has led various writers to study the different terms used to name things and whether or not words have some intrinsic meaning.

Numerous scholars have dealt with language and its relationship with reality. Philosophers, sociologists, linguists, and communication experts have analyzed this topic in detail, although seemingly they primarily studied the "message" sent via any one medium. Among the most important intellectuals who influenced McLuhan's theory was Plato. For instance, Plato's work the *Cratylus, or The Correctness of Names* he presented a detailed analysis of naming practices:

> **Socrates**
>
> How can we assert that they gave names or were lawgivers with knowledge, before any name whatsoever had been given, and before they knew any names, if things cannot be learned except through their names?
>
> **Cratylus**
>
> I think the truest theory of the matter, Socrates, is that the power which gave the first names to things is more than human, and therefore the names must necessarily be correct.[112]

Plato explored what sort of criteria was used for choosing the name for any object. I should note that when speaking about names, such labels make use of words, nouns, adjectives, proper nouns, and language in general.[113] There were mainly interlocutors in Plato's essay; Hermogenes and Cratylus. According to Aristotle, the latter had some influence on Plato's early philosophy.

Hermogenes's position was a conventional one, while Cratylus adopted a naturalist one. Thus, the former believed that naming each object involved local or national conventions, determining what words must be used to indicate particular objects. In this view, the same objects may have different names according to the persons subscribing to conventionalism. Whereas, Cratylus maintained that names could not be chosen arbitrarily through conventionalism because they "naturally" belonged to specific objects. Therefore, he believed that when one speaks about an unnaturally named object, this merely indicated

---

112   Plato, *Cratylus* 438b 5 – 438c 4 (Web. www.perseus.tufts.edu, Plato in Twelve Volumes, Vol. 12 translated by Harold N. Fowler. Cambridge, MA, Harvard University Press; London, William Heinemann Ltd. 1921

113   Web. November 21, 2012 http://plato.stanford.edu/entries/plato-cratylus/

an object as something it was not. For example, calling Socrates "Hermogenes" would lead to an error, as this name did not correspond to him.

It is challenging to maintain a naturalist position regarding names. By asserting such a position, one would seem to imply that humans are capable of knowing the essence of things and their name. The problem with that approach is that is does not accept knowledge of reality as it is, but instead a name avowed "by nature." Nevertheless, Plato's position was interesting in that, to him, a "name" must definitively relate in some way to the thing it named. He saw a name as a significant symbol of the relationship between humans and the world. We must also keep in mind that Plato was under the impression that things had a consistent self of their own. For him, things did not relate nor depend upon us, and they did not allow themselves to be dragged up or down by the work of our imagination. Instead, they were -- in and of themselves -- related to their own being, according to their nature.[114] Hence, the importance of humans determining a name based on a thing's essence. If a term used to call a thing was accidental, we would be running the risk of losing a name-thing relationship, since accidents are capable of getting lost or changing at any time, while a thing remains. Thus. a name manifests something not in movement or circulation, but rather at rest; meaning, a permanent unchanging definition as is. Therefore, Socrates upheld that a name was an instrument that imparted and distinguished essence, as its own name indicated:

> The words τὸ ὄν (being) and οὐσία (*ousía*) (existence) agree with ἀληθής (*aléthés*) (truth) with the loss of iota, for they mean "going" (ἰόν). And οὐκ ὄν (not being) means οὐκ ἰόν (not going), and indeed some people pronounce it so.[115]

On the other hand, to him, naming depended on reality, on its environment to manifest itself and be understood. To Socrates, naming also influenced human behavior being that a name resulted in what humans are capable of understanding about reality. Lastly, it should be noted that he saw names or words as a medium for the development of reason, *logos*, with which humans formalize reality. This is further expanded upon later, in congruence with McLuhan 's phrase that "the medium is the message." Said again, every medium developed in our world, and primarily language, determines our being, culture, and society in some way, making this research relevant.

Thus, for Marshall McLuhan, the doctrine of names was given through

---

114 *Cratylus* 386e
115 *Cratylus* 421b-c

language—and not a simple theory of oral terminology—but of the essence.[116] To him, the importance of language, or rather of names, could not be dealt with only as a mere convention through which a system of symbols gave way to a determined term or concept. Rather, language must be referred to and studied as formal cause indicating a real being of things existing within the world. For McLuhan, this understanding was essential for the world and humans to be linked, without being corrupted by subjectivism and error, that he believed lead to wrong behavior in an unknown world.

In this regard, McLuhan agreed with Plato's position about the relationship between names and their connection to an essence of reality. In *Cratylus*, Plato explained this relationship in detail.

For Plato, names contained a measure of conventionalism, but not entirely. He thought this was evidenced by the etymology of words, that demonstrated that names were not arbitrary, but coded descriptions of an object. In *Cratylus*, Socrates provided several further examples as to how even people's names related to their origin. Although it would be difficult to determine the actual creation of each name, considering that it would require someone to go back to the origins of civilization. However, finding traces is tenuous because there is no clear evidence, due to a lack of determined speech. Still, Socrates reflected on the origin of some names to illustrate his point:

> Something of this sort, then, is what I suspect: I think the earliest men in Greece believed only in those gods in whom many foreigners believe today— sun, moon, earth, stars, and sky. They saw that all these were always moving in their courses and running (*the/onta*), and so they called them gods (*theou/j*) from this running (*thei/n*) nature; then afterwards, when they gained knowledge of the other gods, they called them all by the same name. Is that likely to be true, or not?[117]

His example outlined how the name "God" was originally related to an essence of his movement. One can identify here the relationship between a name and reality, determining the concept behind the names of beings. We have since kept the name "God" or "Theos" in reference to a higher power, even if the essential idea is not in inference to movement in the modern context. The essence is perfection, which means lack of movement for some[118] and

---

116 See: McLuhan Marshall. *The Classical Trivium: The Place of Thomas Nashe in the Learning of His Time.* Gingko Press, CA 2006 p. 16
117 *Cratylus* 397c-d
118 Aristotle noted that God, or the Prime Mover, must be a perfect entity, totally lacking movement since it would imply imperfection and, therefore, could not be named God. Catholicism adopted some Aristotelian assumptions to explain divinity, even if the theme

continuous movement for others. Another example was the case of Heroes in the *Cratylus*:

> Why, they were all born because a god fell in love with a mortal woman, or a mortal man with a goddess. Now if you consider the word "hero" also in the old Attic pronunciation you will understand better; for that will show you that it has been only slightly altered from the name of love (*Eros*), the source from which the heroes spring, to make a name for them.[119]

In addition, regarding humans, Socrates said:

> The name "man" (*Anthropos*) indicates that the other animals do not examine, or consider, or look up at any of the things that they see, but man has no sooner seen—that is, *opope*—than he looks up at and considers that which he has seen. Therefore, of all the animals man alone is rightly called man (*Anthropos*), because he looks up at what he has seen (*opope*).[120]

As stated in the quote above, during ancient times, the difference between humans and all other living beings was clear between philosophers. Perhaps it was Aristotle who explained in most detail what being human implied and what he argued the essential characteristics of a human being were. Nevertheless, before said great Greek philosopher, humanness was emphasized by male intellectuals as those with the ability to reflect, distinguishing themselves from animals. Again, human reflection was considered as an essential aspect of humanness, upon which our naming and self-advocacy capacities depended. It should also be noted that male humans were considered political animals in the Aristotelian sense, making their ability to converse even more clear. But a negative aspect of ancient Greece was that cishet women were not considered political animals. Women were seen as objects that were owned by cishet men, deemed incapable of such reflections.

Lastly, let us cite the case of the term "body":

> I think this admits of many explanations, if a little, even very little, change is made; for some say it is the tomb (σῆμα) (*sema*) of the soul,

---

of movement is no longer an essential characteristic of God since creation could not be explained without God.
119 *Cratylus* 398d
120 *Cratylus* 399c

their notion being that the soul is buried in the present life; and again, because by its means the soul gives any signs which it gives, it is for this reason also properly called "sign" (σῆμα) (sema).

Reflecting on this quote, there appeared to be a certain difficulty in detecting the origins of embodiment. As we can see, it might have meant two different things. Although, in this case, both meanings had to do with the essence of the named thing. However, Socrates illustrated how seeking the origin of a name could many times lead to a false meaning, due to a lack of evidence from the past that could point us towards a correct hermeneutic of the same. In *Cratylus*, Plato indicated that this term may have been coined by Orpheus and his followers; mainly, in relation to his notion that the soul cleansed guilt. In addition, he described the body, as an enclosure that kept the soul safe, while imprisoning it. Thus, as the name itself denoted, thie body was the *soma* (safe) for the soul, "until the penalty is paid and not even a letter needs to be changed."[121] Theoretically, Pythagorean and Orphic beliefs made a clear influence on these concepts of the soul and body, not only philosophically, but also religiously and politically. For instance, in his age, Pythagoras was an immensely important ancient philosopher known for numerous theories. The most significant ones being those that traversed the concerns discussed in this section in an anthropological fashion.

Names are media that comprise a certain content, but it also tells us more than just what the thing is. In the example of the word *soma*, it is already charged with information which is transferred to the named object, linking to it. In this case, the body implies a prison, leading to the notion that the soul is enclosed in it. Thus, the word has to do with the essence, as well as with a religious, anthropological, ethical, and psychological idea, thus impacting humans and society. When we name something, we are already bound to make certains assumptions about it. This implies that efficient cause and formal cause relate to the name, as well as its origin, and the essence of the being to which it refers. This denotes importance of formal cause in the naming of things, in accordance with an Aristotelian dialogue that claimed formal cause states what the thing is in this way. A name manifests being, based on a definition, Thus, logically, Aristotle would advocate for the naturalistic position regarding origin of names, as well as McLuhan's theory on media as society's formal cause. Keeping in mind, words alter thoughts about an indicated thing.

The subject of the origin of names leads us to wonder: who were the first humans to have named things? What was the first language used for naming? Can one talk about a primeval language or of various tongues? These

---

121   *Cratylus* 340c

questions have preoccupied several scholars, both ancient and contemporary. Namely, the Greek historian Herodotus told of an experiment carried out by Psammetichus, the Ancient Egyptian Pharaoh (fifth century BC), who aimed to discover which humanoid was the first to create language. In this experiment, he randomly chose two newborn babies and handed them over to the care of a goatherd, under strict instructions to feed them goat's milk and isolate them from any human contact, so that no human word would reach the little ones' ears. The king hoped that by doing this, the children would yield to their natural impulses and utter their first words, artificially recreating the first language generation of the original humanoids. As the story goes, according to Herodotus, his experiment was a success. After two years of this child's isolation, the keeper opened the door to the child's hut to give them some goat milk, and they reached out, crying "*Bekos.*" The goatherd reported this to the king, and, following an investigation, the king discovered that *bekos* was the Phrygian word for bread. He then concluded that the Phrygians were the first humanoid from which language emerged. In another experiment, two children were isolated together with a mute woman on the island of Inchkeith, and she was ordered to stay there until they reached the age of perfect speech. It is said that these children spoke Hebrew, although the chronicler had some doubts about it.[122] What was certain is that the subject of speech and names drew the attention of different disciplines because of the questions above.

Furthermore, "names" of things have evolved over time. Early nations named things using terms tightly related to reality, but as society developed, so did speech, becoming increasingly abstract. As such, meaning of words drifted farther from reality. Today, there is no codification that clearly links the proximity of names to the things or their essence, as was the case in antiquity.

Therefore, if we had to answer to Plato about whether or not names are dicated by social conventions, we would have to say that today, they are. Names have definitely changed and evolved as did the societies in which they were created. Moreover, names are media, and are forms that humans created to transmit knowledge or ideas, further developing societal environments.

Words and Subject

To further develop this topic, we should call attention to Ivor Armstrong Richards, another writer who showed the importance of language as a medium of communication and influenced Marshall McLuhan. In 1923, he proclaimed in his book *The Meaning of Meaning* that grammar and language are not independent of the subjects who use them. Said differently, he insisted that

---

[122] Chomsky William. *Hebrew: The Eternal Language.* Varda Books, Illinois 2001, p. 33

"Words 'mean' nothing by themselves." As in, the meaning of words always depends upon how they are contextually used. "It is only when a thinker makes use of them that they stand for anything, or, in one sense, have 'meaning.' They are instruments." Therefore, our thinking controls our words and decides their meaning based on the context used.[123] According to Richards, names depended on something else since, by themselves, they were merely an abstraction. Without their reference to reality, words have no meaning. That is why, yet again, the link between them and the world must be known; otherwise, we cannot communicate nor name anything. One needs a clear and objective foundation regarding "the being" or "the essence" of things. In addition, names depend on humans to be used. And according to Richards, they are media conveying a message that must refer to a context and subject; only then does whatever is said have meaning. Otherwise, it would only consist of loose words that would have no meaning or sense, without any reference.

In his work, Richards emphasized mainly the "way" in which terms are used because, although they are important, words can be used in a variety of ways. In *The Philosophy of Rhetoric*, he put forward that the study of rhetoric should be a philosophical investigation on how words function in speech because a traditional view reduced rhetoric to the subject of persuasion, losing sight of a crucial problem: the function of language. For Richards, rhetoric should be seen as a philosophical discipline aimed at dominating the fundamental laws of language use.[124] He believed this because what we observed that what came to understand about an object's use depended upon the way we used words and names. His observation,, once again, illustrated the medium's importance over the message, since words are tools, or "media," that carry certain information influencing their reception. No matter the gravity of content a sender desires to convey to someone, it has no meaning for others if it cannot be communicated. In more abstract terms, the concept implies matter and form. A concept is itself "form," gaining significance only through its relation to matter, which also depends on the "medium" in order to be communicated. This concept or form is paramount in communication; what is understood by the subject who receives the message depends on it. Repeatedly, we can agree with Marshall McLuhan that "the medium is the message." Words carry information; without them, there is no communication, and we would not be able to express to others what our senses perceive, nor would there be any communication directed towards us because without language, there is no thought. How could we know anything

---

123   See: Ogden, C.K.; Richards, I. A. *The Meaning of Meaning*. Harcourt, Brace and World. Inc. New York, 1927 p. 9-10.

124   See: Hochmuth-Nichols, Marie. "I. A. Richards and the New Rhetoric", *Quarterly Journal of Speech*, 44, pp. 1-16

without names, or without terms? The medium is of great significance, both for informing and memorizing.

Ivor Armstrong Richards also referred to what he called "The Proper Meaning Superstition," which was a conceptualization he used to describe the generalized belief that a word had a proper meaning, regardless of its use. A naturalist view can be detected here, regarding the link between words and reality. According to this, the proper meaning of a word controlled its use and the purpose with which it was articulated. The basis of this superstition was a certain stability in the meaning of some words, which became taken for granted naturalized claim to stability about the meaning of a word. This idea was derived from a persistently reified context that gave it meaning, even though over time all context varies, therefore, transforming the concept.[125] Richard's idea influenced Marshall McLuhan's understanding of language and of how different media of communication transformed our concepts of reality. According to Richards, there are other elements of words involved in understanding of a message: usage and context. As he stated:

> The effects upon the organism due to any sign, which may be any stimulus from without, or any process taking place within (...) Thus when we strike a match, the movements we make, and the sound of the scrape are present stimuli. But the excitation which results is different from what it would be had we never struck matches before. Past strikings have left, in our organization, engrams, residual traces, which help to determine what the mental process will be.[126]

Context leads us to perceive certain messages that may or may not be present in reality. Our ability to think relies on our environments that suggest content, such as in Richards' match example quoted above. However, these ambiguous signs may lead us to mistaking the message.

Richards' claims also showed that language mediated our experience of reality, and in turn, this mediation formed part of our routine. Therefore, the acquisition of a language transformed the speaker's experience of the world. And, so, experiences vary according to the language and way it is used. The Richards quote highlighted two aspects that relate to McLuhan's theory, the subject of this study. One of them concerned the kind of language used, linking this practice to location, era, customs, etc., speech, words, or language change.

---

125 See: Richards, I. A. *Selected Essays* (1929-1974), Oxford University Press, New York 1991, pp. 74-76.
126 See: Ogden, C.K.; Richards, I. A. *The Meaning of Meaning*, Harcourt, Brace and World. Inc. New York, 1927 , p. 52

This affected the individual's understanding of their medium and relationship with it, and with the society around them. Likewise, Harold Innis's analysis of language extended the study of this aspect, then influencing Marshall McLuhan.

On the other hand, we know language also influences the way a medium is used; words can modify the meaning of what is understood, whether through grammar, rhetoric, or dialectics.

Orality and *Trivium*

In a very detailed analysis of the "use" of language, Marshall McLuhan attested that the world is a book that must be read and transmitted via language, another medium comprised of names, or words. In *The Classical Trivium*,[127] he stressed that this reading could be carried out in three different ways. Based on this very in-depth study, McLuhan attempted to illustrate how different ways of explaining reality develop into a mental structure that configured societies in different historical eras and locations, the former of which we will unpack more in depth below.

According to McLuhan, the first approach to reality was grammar. He said we grasped reality through language in order to transform it into words and thus, be able to communicate it to others. In this sense, Marshall McLuhan detailed an allegorical exegesis of natural phenomena.[128] In addition, for him, language was one of the first media through which humans began transmitting their knowledge of the world and becoming conscious of it. The oldest known examples were the Greek poets Homer and Hesiod (approx. seventh and sixth centuries BC). Based on poetry, as oral culture, they conveyed their interpretations of the world to the ancient Greeks, who were taught to understand reality based on collective memory. We will analyze orality's impact on society below.

Based upon Hesiod and Homer, the main aspects stressed in antiquity were harmony and limit since their works were sung in meter and rhythm. These poets did not limit themselves to describing facts but sought causes and reasons, often of a mythic-fantastic variety. Otherwise, they depicted reality as it was. An example of these characteristics can be seen in the following text:

---

[127] Marshall McLuhan's 1942 doctoral thesis, published for the first time in 2006, on the Trivium, a word in Latin meaning "three paths" which in the Middle Ages the three sciences that comprised it, grammar, rhetoric, and dialectics, were the basis of liberal arts education. McLuhan Marshall. *The Classical Trivium: The Place of Thomas Nashe in the Learning of His Time*. Gingko Press, CA 2006

[128] McLuhan Marshall. *The Classical Trivium: The Place of Thomas Nashe in the Learning of His Time*. Gingko Press, CA 2006, p. 16

You are steeped in insolence and lust of gain. With what heart can any of the Achaeans do your bidding, either on foray or in open fighting? I came not warring here for any ill the Trojans had done me. I have no quarrel with them. They have not raided my cattle nor my horses, nor cut down my harvests on the rich plains of Phthia; for between me and them there is a great space, both mountain and sounding sea. We have followed you, Sir Insolence! for your pleasure, not ours—to gain satisfaction from the Trojans for your shameless self and for Menelaus. You forget this, and threaten to rob me of the prize for which I have toiled, and which the sons of the Achaeans have given me. Never when the Achaeans sack any rich city of the Trojans do I receive so good a prize as you do, though it is my hands that do the better part of the fighting. When the sharing comes, your share is far the largest, and I, forsooth, must go back to my ships, take what I can get and be thankful, when my labor of fighting is done. Now, therefore, I shall go back to Phthia; it will be much better for me to return home with my ships, for I will not stay here dishonored to gather gold and substance for you.[129]

With that said, this exegesis has its pros and cons. Likewise, it may be interpreted in various ways, according to one's understanding of the period, beliefs, customs, and trends. This multiplicity was advantageous to the practice of poetics because it made the style more accessible and easy for all to understand, yet there was room for subjectivity. Meaning, people understood what they wanted within the limits of what they knew. It might also lead to relativism, which would be less advantageous, as reality would be compromised; eliminating prior boundaries of denoted understanding. This process could incline a receiver to lose sight of being, the meaning of reality itself, the world, and/or things being described. There would no longer be any possibility of knowing nature in these circumstances, and the media we have to access to could become useless. However, studying orality enables a closer understanding of antiquity, given that the knowledge obtained through this medium was comprised of concepts accepted without reflection or criticism. Life in oral societies cannot be understood within today's communicative standards. As already stated, a more exhaustive analysis about learning and comprehension is eye-opening.

The second kind of author who, according to Marshall McLuhan, used grammar as a method to read the world, were pre-Socratic philosophers, such as Thales of Miletus, Empedocles, and Zeno of Citium. These intellectuals

---

129 *The Iliad*, Book I. Translated by Samuel Butler. http://classics.mit.edu/Homer/iliad.html

78 | *Formal Cause in Marshall McLuhan's Thinking*

made robust arguments in efforts to explain the world. However, their type reasoning would not have been possible without the initial development of Homeric poems, which enabled male-centric human thinking to develop and reach a higher level of abstraction than that of Homer and Hesiod's era. Thales, for example, argued that water was the beginning of all reality, as it made up every being. While Empedocles amended that movement and structure could not be explained by a single element. Further, his position was that initially, there were four elements: water, air, fire, and earth, as these constituted the world around us.

Another example that expanded on this line of thought came from Stoic philosophers. For them, there was a universal "Reason" (*Logos*)[130] ordering absolutely everything, from nature to human thinking, so much so, that they believed this *Logos* was a necessary condition in understanding the world, which they described as perpetually in motion: *panta rhei*.[131] To them, those who did not grasp that concept could not obtain truth, meaning essential knowledge of life.

Their explanation was not based upon philosophical arguments alone. They also inquired into whether or not humans' knowledge of the world was real, leading us to two quandaries: first, the form transmitting this knowledge, and second, its matter, whether it was true or not. For this school of thought, the only guarantee would have been an entity separate from human beings and the world, giving order and enabling humans to understand it. Also, this correlation would guarantee that humans were able to read the book of nature, which would indicate that order was also contained in the world. If the stoics were correct, we could assert that language would be "the effect of reason,"[132] as well as the medium, par excellence, with which we exchange information.

---

130   One can speak of two important times as of the appearance of this philosophical school of thought. The first, the times of its founder, Zeno of Citium, at the end of the Hellenistic period, between 324 and 262 BC. The second, during the Roman Empire, at the times of Lucius Annaeus Seneca, from 4 BC to 65 AD, Epictetus, from 55 to 135 AD, and Marcus Aurelius, from 121 to 180 AD. This term was considered as the opposite of myth in Hellenistic times, and was later translated by the Romans as "reason" and "speech," although in contemporary times, the notion of "universal law" or of "the laws of nature" have been included. See: McLuhan Marshall. *The Classical Trivium: The Place of Thomas Nashe in the Learning of His Time*. Gingko Press, CA 2006 p. 22

131   For Marshall McLuhan, this idea seems to have been the influence of Heraclitus of Ephesus, "The Obscure," who alleged that everything was in constant flow and that the same thing could not be known at different times. His famous phrase in the philosophical field is *panta rhei* ("everything flows"). As times goes by, things change constantly, making it is impossible to see the "same" person at two different times.

132   See: McLuhan Marshall. *The Classical Trivium: The Place of Thomas Nashe in the Learning of His Time*. Gingko Press, CA 2006 p. 26

Understanding the world through the second component, grammar, would be most appropriate. In this view, with adequate, truth-led argumentation, philosophy could maintain the world's objectivity to ensure the perpetuity of being through research.

An additional means of understanding the world is through dialectics, which origins lie with Zeno of Elea: "Zeno´s method, defined which such exact precision, is what, since Aristotle, has been called the "dialectical."[133] According to some ancient Greeks, dialectics, could be applied to any object of reality, whether inert or alive. Procedurally, it was a series of questions and answers, related to general matters, and as a part of endoxa.[134] Methodically, male Greek intellectuals believed that statements should be presented as true because they stemmed from experts on the subject, and this approach demonstrated consistent arguments.[135] In this way, Aristotle, in *Organon*[136] showed the many possibilities existed in this system of reasoning and the variables that lead an interlocutor to adequate thought processes.[137] At its core, dialectics was meant to source the essence of things via *logos*: "The dialectician reaches the limit of the intelligible, just as the prisoner released from the cave,"[138] opposed to grammar, which was limited to an interpretation of natural phenomena, whether through myths or via a philosophical explanation of causal force, as above. However, these methods do not reach a truth of natural phenomena like dialectics does, through means of criticizing statements given to confirm their truth or show their falsehood, e.g., following the dialectical process, shown by Plato in *Phaedrus*:

> I hypothesize the logos which I judge to be strongest and whatever seems to me to agree with it I set down as really so - whether with regard to causes or anything else; and what does not, as not so.[139]

In his own work, Marshall McLuhan also indicated that the development of dialects offered a different approach to reality, triggered through the methods of Sophist philosophers,[140] who during the fifth Century BC attempted

---

133 *Ibid* p. 39
134 Credible opinions of experts on the subject.
135 Web. http://plato.stanford.edu/entries/aristotle-rhetoric/#dialectic
136 A collection of works on logic.
137 Aristotle here means that this system is good in relation to form, in the sense that it can lead us more assuredly to the truth of reality.
138 See Plato's *Republic* VII, 532b 2 in Sayre, Kenneth M. *Plato´s Literary Garden: How to Read a Platonic Dialogue*. University of Notre Dame Press, 1995. p. 131
139 *Phaedrus*, 100a 3-7
140 The Greek word *Sophistes*, formed from the noun *Sophia*, meaning wisdom, relates to

to teach rhetoric in a similar way to how philosophers of that time taught dialectics. Thus, these approaches have clashed in an intellectual battle, since the time of Athens, during which one was deemed right or wrong based on their argumentation; without an added need for scientific evidence—simply persuasion—they convinced an audience.

At times, the dialectical process has been confused with rhetorical criticism since both are based on arguments used to develop a defense of certain theses. Nevertheless, they are very different. As a method, dialectics can be applied to any object, and most simply is a series of questions and answers. It deals with general subjects, part of endoxa (credible opinions) that have been confirmed by experts and proven by arguments. In turn, traditional rhetoric not only dealt with strong arguments and proof, but also with male credibility and emotional attitudes. This rhetoric was a part of endoxa, but belonged to the (male) public in general. Even though both dialectics and rhetorical criticism may converge in discussing similar objects, their methods also differ. Dialectics necessitated production of scientific knowledge supported by arguments, while rhetoric's raison d'être was to enact artistic persuasion, swaying an audience on a specific thesis.

This distinction between the approaches is important because Sophists demonstrated how rhetoric can often overpower dialectics, through the use of "Sophist" arguments and/or the power of persuasion. Hence why to them, dialectics was lesser than rhetoric since the spoken word was seen as stronger than ever before; words did not depend on reality anymore. Instead, reality depended on them somehow, being that words named what things were. However, philosophers, like Plato and Aristotle, denied this position, arguing that rhetoric was secondary to dialectics. They insisted that technically, words were based on reality, and that it was where truth existed, not words, which were changeable, like the multitude of subjects expressed in them. Marshall McLuhan mentioned this when he said that "the history of the trivium is largely a history of the rivalry among them for ascendancy."[141]

In this sense, Marshall McLuhan focused on grammar since both dialectics and rhetoric are based on language. Without it, neither would have emerged. He based himself on science which primarily expresses what reality is and

---

those who practice wisdom or teaching. The Sophist philosophers first became known in the fifth century BC, as a new kind of intellectuals or teachers who offered education to the Greek, especially in public speaking and life conduct. For some, the Sophists were an extension of the traditional rhapsodists of that time, but dedicated to areas of interest of the era. They were also a response to the cultural, social, political, and financial developments of that period. See: Web. http://plato.stanford.edu/entries/sophists/

141 See: McLuhan Marshall. *The Classical Trivium: The Place of Thomas Nashe in the Learning of His Time.* Gingko Press, CA 2006 p. 42

shows reality's essence via language, so that humans can understand it. In each era, both dialectics and rhetoric became "modes" of explanation about the world. Clearly, only under these conditions would grammar be superior to dialectics and rhetoric, as it is the basis for both methods. However, it seems to me that grammar is not enough today, since according to Richards, "words" in themselves mean nothing.[142] Instead, their meaning always depends on "how they are used." Only when a thinking subject uses them do they represent something or have any meaning; they are tools. Therefore, thinking controls words, determining their sense based on the context in which they are used. Hence the centrality of the methodical medium used to understand the world, whether that be, in this case, dialectics and/or rhetoric.

As has been detailed above, understanding is partially determined by the way language is used. Historically, in the case of grammar, humans have been able to conceptualize the world around them, as this was the first step towards developing an increasingly more specific vocabulary, adapting into various media of communication. Rhetoric came after, allowing human beings to argue their opinions and beliefs, using emotions to convince or persuade an opponent. Lastly, came dialectics, with which much more abstract thinking was developed, and rules of thought were formulated, leading humans to focus more on themselves and less on the world.

Another integral writer to the development and analysis of language, as a modifier of society, was Harold Adams Innis. He greatly influenced Marshall McLuhan's theory. The latter himself explicated as much in *The Gutenberg Galaxy*—that Innis was the first to perceive changes in media's technology[143]. Thus, Innis's theory of communications are of importance to this study.

Language and Its Relation to the Development of Culture

Throughout history, societies have undergone various changes due to the kind of communication that were introduced into them. This was a theory that Harold Innis put forward. In it, he emphasized the development of speech and written language as a basis of societal changes.

According to Innis, the rise and fall of civilizations, as well as cultural changes can be understood as functions of the predominant communication media, because civilizations develop at a certain time and space; therefore, they

---

142 See Ogden, C.K., Richards, I. A. *The Meaning of Meaning*. Harcourt, Brace and World. Inc. New York, 1927, p. 28.
143 Hernández Juan Abelardo. *Rationality in Marshall McLuhan and the Toronto School*. Doctoral thesis, Universidad Panamericana, 2004, p. 19 (in Spanish)

can be analyzed according to their space and duration:

> A medium of communication has an important influence on the dissemination of knowledge over space and over time and it becomes necessary to study its characteristics in order to appraise its influence in its cultural setting. According to its characteristics it may be better suited to transportation, or to the dissemination of knowledge over space and over time, particularly if the medium is light and easily transported. The relative emphasis on the time or space will imply a bias of significance to the culture in which it is imbedded.[144]

The distinction made by Innis illustrated the importance of media of communication in relation to societal changes and destruction, as he described in one of his works entitled *Empire and Communications*. He also distinguished between two kinds of media, each with its own bias that he said were responsible for changes. One kind related to time, associated with durable and heavy media like stone or clay tablets, being that they were of substantial weight and difficult to move, and inhibited spatial expansion. However, these durable objects also enabled a culture's resilience, despite the passage of time. Innis also linked this kind of bias to an emphasis on rituals and customs, as well as other cultural practices deemed sacred and moral. One must remember that cultures that spanned centuries, for example, like Egyptian and Jewish ones, had significant moral and religious components. He argued time bias also favored the development of social hierarchies, as was seen throughout Egypt's history. Lastly, for Innis, speech was associated with a bias towards time as well. He also explained that the bias was space specific. To him, this bias consisted of light and portable media that could be transported over long distances. This related to secular and territorial societies because they facilitated the spatial expansion of empires. This was evidenced in Roman culture, which unlike the Egyptians, spread throughout Europe and parts of Asia and Africa. Paper, for example, was an easily transportable medium with a relatively short life span.

As follows, Innis was convinced that media and their biases were important for the development or decadence of a culture, as well as for its stability, which was achieved by sustaining a balance between biases of space and time. He also believed that changes came from the margins of society because due to their distance from the center, they tended to develop their own media. Therefore, new media empowered those at the margins to develop and consolidate a certain power, sometimes reaching the center and changing authority. Accordingly, we

---

144   Innis Harold. *The Bias of Communication*. Toronto Press, Canada 1951, p. 33

should primarily pay attention to these kinds of media, as social changes depend on them. Lastly, Innis reflected on technology-based social conditioning, referring to the tools we use in our daily lives.

Building upon this legacy, Marshall McLuhan recognized the importance and predominance of Innis's theory. He described how writing on paper instead of on stone tablets revolutionized human history. In *Empire and Communications*, Innis indicated that militarism stemmed from papyrus, since the latter facilitated message exchange. He argued the fall of the Roman Empire came about when papyrus dried out. Consequently, he alleged novel communication tools arose, giving rise to new civilizations. Innis also noted the importance of analyzing each medium to understand its characteristics and how it was used and received in society. Thus, Innis saw a relationship between society and technology.[145]

An overview of his work helps reveal the fundamental role that language plays in human life. If Innis was correct, when language emerged, thinking was then founded upon the use of it, and, this alteration irreparably transformed proceeding human capabilities to think without language. This is because when referring to a real object, we use a medium, allowing us to speak about it. Form determines matter, content, and this caused a change in the individual and society.

The medium, not reality, is our reference, since the latter presents itself to us via the name.

> One way or another, we can assert that words are complex systems of metaphors and symbols that translate experience into our pronounced or externalized senses. By translating immediate sensory experiences into vocal symbols, the entire world can be recalled and retrieved at any time.[146]

Through the use of language, we can name anything that exists in our world; we can recognize it and manifest it to others without having it before us. Thus, "form"—the medium—is more important than the content, just as Marshall McLuhan stated. Language impacts not only reality itself, but also the human being who perceives that reality. The effects of language on humans have changed human rationality.

---

145 Soules Marshall. *The Bias of Communications & Monopolies of Power*. 1996. Web May 5, 2013. http://www.media-studies.ca/articles/innis.htm
146 McLuhan Marshall. *Understanding Media: the Extensions of Man*. MIT Press, London 1994, p. 69

Speech and Its Relation to Mimesis

As discussed, the history of patriarchal civilizations has been documented as a battle between speech (hearing) and written language (sight). Many ancient rhapsodies have recited human history based upon an understanding of language, like Homer's and Hesiod's stories, since:

"Language is deeply entangled in the spiritual evolution of mankind, it accompanies the latter at every stage of its local advance or retreat, and the state of culture at any time is also recognizable in it."[147]

With language, humans have been able to convey their experiences, ideas, and tales of the past, on the assumption that there was another human capable of understanding what they would say, who would receive their explanation as part of their experience. In order for this process to be carried out, dialogue presupposed an existence of language. Through the medium of words, we can recognize other societies, and even interpret how they existed and acquired culture over time.

The influence of speech on society can be seen clearly reflected in the cultural literature of ancient Greece. During that time, young people, women, nor the elderly were allowed to read books, whether for education or leisure. They could not acquire knowledge by buying *The Iliad* and taking it home to read the way people are able to today. At the time, there were books, of course, and the alphabet had been in use for approximately three hundred years,[148] but there was no public access to these works. As stated, women were seen by men as objects to be owned by them, and therefore the majority were not taught to read or write. Beyond them, the majority of the population was also not taught these skills. It is, therefore, fascinating to ask ourselves what the role of writing was then, and what the reasons there were for humans deemed less than elite men of ancient times to be excluded from written works, reserved by men for only a small selection of other literate men. For example, male poets wrote for their own benefit, increasing and improving their composition abilities. However, they composed for audiences who could not read, but listen to their artistic compositions. Therefore, these male poets writings were for themselves. Poetry was a subjective medium that enabled them to remember the content and how to express it:

It is certain that all his [Homer's] poet successors were writers. But it is

---

147 Humboldt Von, Wilhelm. *On Language: On the Diversity of Human Language Construction and its Influence on the Mental Development of the Human Species.* Cambridge University Press, New York 1999, p. 24

148 Havelock Eric. *Preface to Plato.* Harvard University Press, USA 1963. p. 38

equally certain that they always wrote for recitation and for listeners. They composed, it can be said, under audience control. The advantages of literacy were private to themselves and their peers. The words and sentences they shaped had to be such as were repeatable. They had to be 'musical' in a functional sense (...). And the content had still to be traditional.[149]

Experts like Eric Havelock noted that according to evidence from the fifth century BC, men of Athens learned how to read in their adolescence, following previous oral training. Although, some may have learned to write little more than their own names.[150] The question that arises about this context is: how, with such little documentation, were Greeks men able to preserve their system? Meaning, how did they retain their public and private laws, property and traditions, sense of history, and technical abilities? How, without writing, did they ensure organization prevailed? For some, the answer was a simple one; the preservation and dissemination of customs were left to the unconscious mind of (predominantly male) community members, passed down from one generation to the next.[151] These societal practices illustrate the influence language has on society and the way this medium allowed the ancient Greeks to preserve their own systems. This did this not in an external medium such as papyrus or clay, but within every citizen, and in this way they practiced the customs, values, and principles, known to Greek society alone. Being that they did not depend on something external, their knowledge was left out reach of people outside the *polis*.

It seems this pattern of knowledge-keeping created group connections. The male knowledge that was retained and transmitted over generations created a shared consciousness and common set of values. However, this could only be preserved as long as the knowledge was deemed objective and distinguished from everyday experience.[152] Their information was preserved in memory, where consciousness was believed to be located. Memory enabled the storage of thoughts and ideas experienced by humans, who could then organize thoughts coherently, conducting complex intellectual processes; the mind could search memory archives and retrieve information. Thus, memory is also a "form," or medium, of human consciousness and the mind.

In addition, memory is not limited to the individual. Memories can be shared; therefore, humans can manifest themselves, their dialogue, and their

---

149   *Ibid* p. 46
150   *Ibid* p. 40
151   *Ibid* p. 41
152   *Ibid* p. 42

memories and experiences with others, whether orally, in writing, or via any other symbol. This also shows that all forms of communication are in some way extensions of memory. Thus, the shared memory of a group or society is called "collective memory." Cultural knowledge is a major part systematic communication, extending collective memory, enabling customs to be passed down to younger generations. In this sense, we transcend time and life limitations through memory. Memories allow for temporal cohesion of societies, by preserving indvidual identities and cultural social relations.

However, in preliterate societies, some theorists believe that a robust and reliable collective social memory was an absolute prerequisite in ability to maintain societal functions. With that said, how could a living memory retain elaborate linguistic principles without incurring change from one person to another, from one generation to the next, and without losing firmness and authority? It seems the only verbal technology could guarantee preservation and fixity of transmission in these kind of societies; the rhythmic word, artfully organized in verbal and metrical patterns unique enough to retain their shape.[153] Thus, music became a crucial medium for the conservation of traditions because its features allowed humans to retain knowledge and pass it down with more precision. This illustrates the importance of what medium is used to preserve information. In this case, the content depends on the medium for its essence not to change. As mentioned, the Greek system's formal cause was rhythm, music. Without it, the essence of the transmitted message would change. Thus, the challenge of orality, as stated by Havelock,[154] is individual subjectivity. But, on the other hand, subjectivity is a necessary condition for human conservation. Therefore, a vessel, a medium, is needed for news to be sent in reflexive detail. "The medium is the message" because the way a tale reaches us implies a vessel. In this case, not only the information stays intact, but also the impact of a medium on humans is different from one to another, as we shall see in the case of written language, and of speech as a medium.

To transmit a society's culture, each male individual deemed human within said society memorized the information exclusively shared with them. This male memorization was carried out through the poetic tradition of purposeful recitation. These actors could not refer to or memorize a book; they had to

---

153   *Ibid* p. 43
154   Eric Alfred Havelock (1903–1988), was a British citizen who lived most of his life in Canada and the United States. He was a University of Toronto professor who actively participated in the Canadian Socialist movement during the thirties. Studies within his ample work that relate to communication, subscribe to the Canadian school of Harold A. Innis and Marshall McLuhan. Havelock not only had a clear influence on McLuhan, but also contributed to the establishment of analytical principles which link media of communication to the formation of knowledge.

learn to without one:

> His Greek counterpart had to mobilize the psychic resources necessary to memorize Homer and the poets, or enough of them to achieve the necessary educational effect. To identify with the performance as an actor does with his lines was the only way it could be done.[155]

This leads us to consider the personal circumstances of each male child or adult who was required to memorize and keep alive the verbal tradition upon which their culture depended. Initially, they would listen and then repeat. They would later continue repeating and growing their mental repertoire, whose limits could vary from one male child to another and from one male adult to another. If we compare modern students to male ancient Greek ones, we can see that today's students pour their energy into reading and learning from books or any other written medium, using their eyes instead of their ears. The difference has to do with the use and attention of various senses. In the case of speech, hearing was the only way men could acquire conceptual knowledge about their male ancestors, and this way of learning entailed listening to others and trusting what they were saying. The spoken medium allowed for a greater intersubjectivity and a closer relationship between each male member, leading to a significantly more cohesive *polis*. Also, written language entails a perception of information by sight, impacting an individual differently—thus, an intersubjective relationship is not needed, and knowledge can be acquired in isolation. Instead of unifying the city through a false claim to a reductive past linguistically constructed and passed down entirely by/to men, reading inclined group divisions. Now, there was not a sole interpretation. What was written into one text could then be read by those taught to read, interpreted differently by each reader, obsolescing memorization since information in text could be read again.

The impact of orality on preliterate cultures was also noticed by philosophers of the age. However, Socrates wrote nothing on this since he thought education should be oral and dialectic, not written and solitary. For Plato, someone also intrigued by the educational process, *mimesis* was a primary resource, necessary for describing the poetic experience. He believed in this so much so that he analyzed in detail how oral education provided a more adequate education of male Greek societial members.[156] Thus, Plato demanded that male intellectuals

---
155   *Ibid* p. 45
156   Havelock describes in detail how Plato showed the importance of mimesis in ancient education. See: HAVELOCK Eric, *Preface to Plato*, Harvard University Press, USA 1963. p. 45

review and reorganize the poetic experience, be reflexive, and separate themselves from language instead of identifying with it. In his view, they should become "subjects," standing apart from an "object" in order to reconsider, analyze, and evaluate it instead of merely "imitat[ing]" them.[157] This exercise was somewhat complex for male poets because their learning processes included both content and enacted rhythmic movements, identifying with the medium and message in an irreflexive way. Realistically, there was no rational justification for these male Greeks to carry tradition, principles, and customs in the ways that they did—they did so because it was their duty as male Greeks, and self-avowed agentic members of an oral community.

In reference to this legacy, Marshall McLuhan proposed that Plato saw the intrusion of mimesis and mythic characters into the brain's right-hemispheric mental theater, casting it as a kind of "psychic poison" or threat to workings of the left hemisphere;[158] its subject, a city-state:

> You threw yourself into the situation of Achilles, you identified with his grief or his anger. You yourself became Achilles and so did the reciter to whom you listened. Thirty years later, you could automatically quote what Achilles had said or what the poet had said about him. Such enormous powers of poetic memorization could be purchased only at the cost of total loss of objectivity. Plato's target was indeed an educational procedure and a whole way of life (…) This kind of drama, this way of reliving experience in memory instead of analyzing and understand it, is for him 'the enemy' (…) This is why the poetic state of mind is for Plato the arch-enemy and it is easy to see why he considered this enemy so formidable. He is entering the lists against centuries of habituation in rhythmic memorized experience.[159]

McLuhan believed Plato's criticism was not fully understood in ancient times because it clashed with the educational tradition of the *polis*. However, both Socrates and Plato, as well as Aristotle at the time, appeared to have

---

157 Havelock Eric. *Preface to Plato*. Harvard University Press, USA 1963. p. 47
158 Marshall McLuhan makes a distinction between two main areas of the brain that have to do with orality and alphabetization: the left hemisphere's organization ability is quantitative (diachronic): reading, writing, organizing within a significant hierarchical parameter. The brain's right hemisphere is the zone of what is qualitative (synchronic), source of what is spatial-tactile, musical and acoustic. When these hemispheric functions are in true balance, which is rare, the result is a "comprehensive knowledge". See: McLuhan Marshall and Powers B. R. *The Global Village: Transformations in World Life and Media in the 21st Century*. New York: Oxford University Press, USA 1989 p. 60
159 Havelock Eric. *Preface to Plato*. Harvard University Press, USA 1963. p. 45, 47

understood the role that the male subject had on the educational process to be who they really were a thinking, political being. Marshall McLuhan also referred to this when he proclaimed that "the medium is the message" because music and rhythm carried certain information that humans repeated without noticing the influence—not the content in itself—but rather of the medium through which information was transmitted. We see this in Plato's criticism. Taking this into consideration, the problem male Greeks had was that they lacked critical thinking at the time they received the information. These men enacted no criticism, no consciousness of the goodness or badness of the principles they were allowed to learn. These men merely repeated what they were told, generation after generation, as if they were living machines.

Plato documented this machine-like behavior in ancient times, attempting to warn the male public. Yet, today we continue to take for granted effects of mass media on our thoughts, actions, and consciousness. The way the mediums, or forms, shape human reason goes unnoticed.

For the male ancient Greeks, epic poems were the vessels, par excellence, to preserve their legitimized words throughout the Dark Ages. There was no more effective way for their traditions to be transmitted clearly; those who listened to their stories and learned them could then repeat them, again and again, reifying their stories using this medium. Thus, epic poetry became the preeminent medium to conserve tradition. Male artists, serving as unconscious vehicles of repetition and recording,[160] were the ideal medium that provoked ways of thinking, molding the era. However, this medium did not endure forever; as humans change, they search for new media.

The end of the Greek Dark Age (circa 1100-750 BC) saw the emergence of Homer and Hesiod, or more concretely, of *The Iliad*, *The Odyssey*, *The Theogony*, and *Works and Days*. The period of orality reached its peak with the appearance of stories told by rhapsodists. Culture and tradition came to be known through the adventures of mythological heroes, and these male tales not only provided male Greeks a feeling of belonging to society, but also gave them their identities:

> Since language, in whatever shape we may receive it, is always the mental exhalation of a nationally individual life, both factors must also enter there as well.[161]

Eric Havelock saw this characteristic as important to the case of media

---

160 Havelock Eric. *Preface to Plato*. Harvard University Press, USA 1963. p. 48
161 Humboldt Von, Wilhelm. *On Language: On the Diversity of Human Language Construction and its Influence on the Mental Development of the Human Species*. Cambridge University Press, New York 1999, p. 49

being that music and rhythm accompanied these stories, reminding that the mind's attention was continually bifocal; it preserves an identity, yet, makes room for difference within one's identity.[162] Meaning, he thought that when humans listen, their intellect enabled them to interpret information transmitted, making it their own, as if coming from another, but, at the same time, knowing it differently. He was confident that minds' take information in accordance with knowledge of personal experiences. However, the medium of the mind is limited; there are a million things that cannot be said in metrical speech. Therefore, they will not be thought about.[163] This limit to speech, in turn, limits human knowledge and access to the truth that male philosophers, primarily Plato, allegedly had. Even he, profoundly criticized educational methods of male Greeks and deemed it most important that men use their intelligence to adopt traditions, laws, and shared principles. Men who do not think and reflect were more like animals, or women, emulating their parents' movements. Formal possession was rationalized by this male form of reason. Therefore, from Socrates' time onwards, the use of dialogue and intersubjective opinions to reach agreement and obtain truth became apparent; this dialogic process enabled men to acquire knowledge consciously. For Plato, reflection was not enough. He sought to get to the root of Greek education to influence society fully. That is why he constantly criticized the Greek teaching method and proposed another one.

Plato knew that, for Greek men, music existed only to make words more memorable or to make the metrical undulations and ripples more effectively recollectable, freeing psychic energy for the recalling of the words themselves.[164] But male Greek education did not limit itself only to rhythmic oral learning. Music also entailed physical movement, which male Greek educators took advantage of in their teaching processes. Therefore, they learned that some physical reflexes could move in conjunction with the movement of the vocal organs: the legs and feet could be organized into dance movements. These moves created a pattern of organized actions whose function was mnemonic. In other words, the body could move to the rhythm of spoken words, spaces, and punctuation and choric recitation became a bodily performance.[165] The message was not only conveyed via the rhythm of the words, but also physically, with the body, too, reciting what the *logos* learned. Both media, melody and dance, served the preservation principle,[166] or so Havelock saw it. Realistically,

---

162   Havelock Eric. *Preface to Plato*. Harvard University Press, USA 1963. p. 147
163   *Ibid* p. 149
164   *Ibid* p. 150
165   *Idem*
166   *Ibid* p. 151

these principles depended on music's mediaticity to such a degree that they were not even viewed as principles, but still followed by humans, the way the body follows music. Thus, Plato's questioning, and later on, Aristotle's were justified—male Greeks who practiced this doctrine did not have to "think" or "reflect" in order to act one way or another. In practice, dance moves made the teaching of the culture and traditions about the *polis* almost second nature in ways male intellectuals took for granted. And even, without them becoming cognizant of the principles.

> The psychological principles governing this elaborate procedures are simple but fundamental. First, all spoken speech is obviously created by physical movements performed in the throat and mouth. Second, in an oral culture, all preserved speech has likewise to be created in this way. Third, it can be preserved only as it is remembered and repeated. Fourth, to ensure ease of repetition, and hints of remembrance, the physical motions of mouth and throat must be organized in a special way. Fifth, this organization consists in setting up patterns of movements which are highly economical (that is, rhythmic). Sixth, these patterns then become automatic reflexes. Seventh, automatic behavior in one part of the body (the voice organs) is been strengthened by parallel behavior in other parts of the body (ears and limbs). The entire nervous system, in short, is geared to the task of memorization.[167]

These elaborate mechanisms of ancient Greek male poetry represented a mobilization of the resources of the unconscious that assisted their conscious. Their goal was for male poets to unconsciously learn the information that favored the development of the *polis*, and this, in some way, contributed to the conscious. Their actions implied they knew that these multipronged enactments and learned instructions could change perceptions of what was morally good or bad. On the other hand, despite the complexity of their interactions, various motor reflexes were so organized that they could operate without any need for the male subject to think while moving. This meant that, not unlike sexual or digestive reflexes, they were highly sensual and were closely linked to physical pleasures. The regularity of dance performance had a hypnotic effect that relaxed mental and physical tensions, anxieties, fears, and uncertainties. They found tiredness could be temporarily forgotten, and, perhaps, erotic impulses stimulated.[168] Again, Marshall McLuhan said that all media are extensions of humans, which cause profound changes in them and their environments.

---

167 *Idem*
168 *Ibid* p. 152

Therefore, the medium was, in turn, the message since information transmitted through it went beyond content. Alone, it was already a message, transforming humanness and society. As an extension, he saw the medium as an amplification of organs, senses, or functions. Linguistically, it was an extension of thought enabling an expression of human ideas, feelings, etc. That is also why Von Humboldt stated that:

> *Language* (...) In itself it is no product (*Ergon*), but an activity (*Energeia*). Its true definition can be only a generic one. For it is the ever-repeated *mental labor* of making the *articulated* sound capable of expressing thought.[169]

Language is a medium that translates reality into symbols, a way of invoking some real subject or object without them or it needing to be present. Ergo, language translates the visual into an abstraction that becomes its name, and limits us to certain words to recall reality, as well as our relationship with other subjects with whom we can effectively communicate through use of words.

For these reasons, Marshall McLuhan proposed that, as an extension of the senses, media caused the human central nervous system to protect the "affected" area by catalyzing a kind of embodied numbness or hypnosis.[170] This is also why many times when using a certain medium, we stop using the sense that has been extended. This process is similar to the one the body undergoes during shock or stress. We lose partial consciousness of what is happening around us.

It has been said that this effect also happens in the case of music:

> In more familiar terms, the Muse, the voice of instruction, was also the voice of pleasure. But the recreation was of a rather special type. The audience found enjoyment and relaxation as they were themselves partly hypnotized by their response to a series of rhythmic patterns, verbal, vocal, instrumental, and physical, all set in motion together and all consonant in their effect.[171]

The Greek resource for the male education of the *polis* involved all human faculties; males were free, as they learned what was instilled in them. They used their senses to perceive, and they imitated what the male poets and rhapsodists showed them. They also enjoyed learning with their passions through the

---

169 Humboldt Von, Wilhelm. *On Language: On the Diversity of Human Language Construction and its Influence on the Mental Development of the Human Species*. Cambridge University Press, New York 1999, p. 49
170 McLuhan Eric, Zingrone Frank. *Essential McLuhan*. Anansi, Toronto 1995, p. 237
171 Havelock Eric. *Preface to Plato*. Harvard University Press, USA 1963. p. 152

physical movements guided by music. This is why Eric Havelock proclaimed that, in this sense, poetry was a possession of mental faculties and not an autonomous exercise.[172]

The previous passage illustrated the fundamental role the medium plays in the exaltation of each faculty, and thus, of the human being (categorized around a Greek male experience), as opposed to the message since, as noted, at the time this was conceived, there was no conscious reflection. Without noticing, male Greeks were educated on virtues, traditions, and customs that did not have nor needed a reason for being, only a link to the medium; a specific metric and rhythm.

They did not carry out these movements with equal strength at all times. For instance, while listening in silence, only their ears were fully engaged. but their ears transmitted messages to their nervous system as a whole. Similarly, their limbs, lips, and throat could also interpret them in silence, just like how their nervous systems, in general, were engaged in what they listened to.[173] This demonstrates the role speech held when the alphabet did not yet impact the majority of people. According to Havelock's research, preliterate people were more engaged in what was said to them than literate societies since what they listened to was a fully embodied experience. When listening, the brain only had to interpret what was said, as opposed to when words were spoken, and people had to carry out at least two actions simultaneously: interpreting and transforming ideas into words.

With all this said, the learning process was not reflective but rather a continuous act of memorization, repetition, and recall, all in action when practicing sentences reinforced by musical and verbal patterns. During performance, the cooperation of all a man's bodily reflexes were enlisted in order to make memorization and repetition more effective. In turn, their reflexes provided an emotional release for the unconscious layers of personality, which could then take control and provide their conscious mind a great deal of relief from tension, fear, and the like. This constituted a hypnotic pleasure of their performance, which put the audience under the male poet's control, but was itself also in service of their educational process. Pleasure was exploited as an instrument of cultural continuity.[174] Another important element during this period was the capacity people have been said to have for direct and sincere actions, as well as for expressing wishes. They were said to have nearly lacked hypocrisy, in ways seemingly impossible to modern society. This might be explained by the learning process through which proprieties of life were

---

172   *Ibid* p. 156
173   *Ibid* p. 152
174   *Ibid* p. 157

taught, that necessitated a high sensual if it was to be effective. In the Greek consciousness, action and diction were linked and inseparable from pleasurable memories.[175] For the era, perhaps Greek education for men was practically their only possibility. There were no other options to choose from, and the experience both male teachers and male students followed informed their pedagogical knowledge. As mentioned before, multiple faculties were involved in their learning, making traditional education pleasurably effective. Therefore, there was a separation between acting and thinking; learning implied both. As we shall see, this all changed once male education utilized the alphabet.

When a male singer recited their traditions, their audiences listened repeatedly to remember what was sung to them. However, the effectiveness of the male singer's repetition depended upon relating the actions and words of the male heroes and embodying them—a process that, once again, took place religiously. In doing so, they also engaged in the repeition and recreation of male traditions with their lips, larynx, and limbs, as well as with the entire apparatus of their unconscious nervous systems. The behavior patterns of the artist and the audience were somewhat identical. These practices could be described as mechanical repetitions of rhythmic actions. Psychologically, these practitioners embodied personal commitment, total surrender, and emotional identification.[176]

Their actions illustrated the influence of one of the first media of humans and society. Speech, as a human development through rationality, led humans to formulate words in order to name reality and create a formal representation of it, not to simply think about images. In this way, due to the creation and naturalization of literacy, we have been able to refer to the world through abstractions and communicate with others to grow rationally. Therefore, Von Humboldt noted:

> There can be nothing present in the soul, save by one's own activity, and understanding and speaking are but different effects of this power of speech. Conversing together is never comparable with the transfer of material. In the understander, as in the speaker, the same thing must be evolved from the inner power of each; and what the former receives is merely the harmoniously attuning stimulus.[177]

Apart from speech manifesting reality and influencing cognitive changes,

---

175   Ibid p. 158
176   Ibid p. 160
177   Humboldt Hon, Wilhelm. *On Language: On the Diversity of Human Language Construction and its Influence on the Mental Development of the Human Species*. Cambridge University Press, New York 1999, p. 57

language also alters interpersonal dynamics, since interactions with others generate opportunities for individual development.

However, as we saw, speech entails some significant consequences that, as its creators, we must identify. Since "the medium is the message," we must realize the medium's implications to our world and ourselves. The naturalization of the spoken word might have made us take for granted what we learn through music, mimesis, and poetic performance, which lead humans to repeat the traditions, customs, and cultural heritage without losing authenticity, also implying a lack of reflection regarding all that is done and thought. According to Plato, this could not be regarded as education, since to him rationality, or reflection regarding acts and thoughts, is what characterized humans. Aristotle would agree with Plato since he believed men should be capable of making sense of what is true and what is false through thought. For him, men should be able to educate other men, and themselves, on worldly truths and their own being, using logic and rhetoric.

For them, the male human form demanded the truth of what one knows; therefore, it was important to analyze whether the information received was true and how much influence the medium had on it. Aristotle also knew about the medium's importance—evidenced by him speaking on logic and rhetoric. From his perspective, the former helped men, those they deemed fully human, reach correct and true conclusions from a given content. The latter used persuasion as a "method" that favored manipulation, but did not ensure the truth, meaning they saw it as an unreliable medium. For Aristotle, form determined content not only in the field of *Physics*, but in communication, and in metaphysics. In this way, he, therefore, coincided with Marshall McLuhan.

In addition, it was explicated by these theorists that form impacted individuals since denial can be supported by false arguments; as can entire societies, manipulating men away from truth.

As has been demonstrated, speech is not a medium par excellence. Even though speech was one of the first and most important mediums for humanity, the emergence of the alphabet and of hand writing significantly changed evolution and individual development throughout history.

Written Language as the Foundation of Individuality

> Languages as human artifacts, collective products of human skill and need, can easily be regarded as "mass media", but many find it difficult to consider the newer media deriving from these languages as new

"languages".[178]

As has been discussed at length in previous sections, language is one of the first media humans used to develop in the world. Through communication, humans developed tools, extended their cognitive capacities, and improved through a manifestion of their internal selves outward. In addition, humans today are capable of noticing the numerous extensions of our cognitive resources, impacting social relations writ large. Therefore, the importance of researching it today is now clear.

Language is for intelligence what the wheel is for the feet and entire body. These symbols enabled travel from one point to another with greater ease, speed, and with less and less bodily involvement and/or exertion necessary to do so. Language extended and broadened the individual but also divided their faculties.[179] It transformed our realities into representations through use of words; the latter being signs that link to reality itself. And, thus, these names language are comprised of, are "media." Through them we are able to know reality, intentionally and abstractly.

In his work *The Global Village*, Marshall McLuhan presented a model for researching the structural impact technologies had on societies. His model emerged from his observations that all media and technologies have had a fundamentally linguistic structure. Said otherwise, to McLuhan these technologies were not just similar to language; in essential form, they were language because they used symbols encoded by humans in order to communicate. This is why he extensively documented ways humanness, as we know it, originated in this ability of humans to extend themselves through their senses towards the environment(s) which surrounded them.[180] Moreover, in this persepcvtive, tools are seen as part of the individual. As Marshall McLuhan indicated, they were an extension of the individual. Therefore, they belonged to the individual and modifyed their way of thinking and acting in the world. "Media," therefore, are the human being's formal cause. They mediate the individual. If we consider humans and their environment holistically, then we must also consider the tools they used as formal cause of said whole because, depending on them, humans "are" one way or another. They modified their essence. Modern humans are not the same as prehistoric humans were, which is

---

178   McLuhan Marshall. "Myth and Mass Media", *Daedalus,* Vol. 88, No. 2, (Spring 1959), p. 339-348

179   McLuhan Marshall. *Understanding Media: the Extensions of Man*. MIT Press, London 1994, p. 91

180   McLuhan Marshall and Powers B. R. *The Global Village: Transformations in World Life and Media in the 21st Century*. Barcelona: Gedisa, 1989 p. 16 (In Spanish)

largely due to the use of certain media, and certain languages.

Marshall McLuhan provided an interesting example illustrating this difference: what would happen if we wrote the words "American Flag" instead of having stars and stripes on a piece of cloth and waved it. While these symbols would express the same meaning, their effects would be very different. The first image would mean something only to literate people who also knew that the words referred to the thing through use of both terms. These symbols are an abstract language that strip away an important part of the image's qualities. On the other hand, the stars and stripes image would be accessible to anyone who can visualize, but similarly, in order to know what the image would be referring to, viewers would need to know what the words were meant to reference.

This example showed some of the differences between the acoustic or illiterate individual and the visual or literate one.

In *Art and Illusion*, Ernst Gombrich pointed out that the difference between signs and images had to do with the different mental dispositions one needed to adopt to understand what was presented. In addition, to Marshall McLuhan, almost all collective and familiar emotions and feelings were eliminated from the social group's relationships once the alphabet was used and the person became emotionally free to break away from the tribe in order to become civilized, e.g., a visually organized individual with attitudes, habits, and rights deemed civilized by other men.[181]

We could ask ourselves whether or not there is a significant difference between these two representations, the one based on imagery and the other which involved symbolics and other naming practices. Even still, there are those who have maintained that there has never been an image of nature as it is, but rather all images are based on conventions, in a similar fashion to written characters. All images are signs; therefore, any science that studies them involves more semiotics than psychology[182] or sociology. It may seem that the difference between these two representations is nothing more than a continuum, being that both are signs that refer to something else, dependent upon our preconceptions of their contextual order and meanings for interpretation.

The phonetic alphabet is a unique technology. Many types of pictographic and syllabic writings have existed prior to it, but there is only one phonetic alphabet in which letters, without semantic sense, correspond to sounds, that are devoid of semantic sense.

Our words separate themselves from reality because they are abstractions,

---

181   McLuhan Marshall. *Understanding Media: The Extensions of Man*. MIT Press, London 1994, p. 23
182   See: Gombrich Ernst H. *Art and Illusion: A Study in the Psychology of Pictorial Representation*. Princeton University Press, N.Y. 1960, Preface.

while reality is believed by some to be something concrete that presents itself to us through images. "Only the phonetic alphabet makes such a sharp division in experience, giving to its user an eye for an ear, and freeing him from the tribal trance of resonating word magic and the web of kinship."[183] Unlike speech, with which we can communicate intersubjectively and with another person idiosyncratically, the phonetic alphabet (implying writing) eliminates a need for "another" with whom to communicate, substituting them with words to "read." In the reading process, reality is transformed from its colorful, particular, and concrete setting into an abstract representation in black and white. Marshall McLuhan also indicated that links between individuals disappear with the phonetic alphabet because direct communication is lost and replaced by an impersonal one.

In "Culture, Psychiatry, and the Written World," published in the November 1959 issue of *Psychiatry*, the renowned twentieth-century ethno-psychiatrist J.C. Carothers investigated several illiterate tribes in Africa and compared them to the people of the Western world to show some significant differences:

> By reason of the type of educational influences that impinge upon Africans in infancy and early childhood, and indeed throughout their lives, a man comes to regard himself as a rather insignificant part of a much larger organism—the family and the clan—and not as an independent, self-reliant unit; personal initiative and ambition are permitted little outlet; and a meaningful integration of a man's experience on individual, personal lines is not achieved. By contrast to the constriction at the intellectual level, great freedom is allowed for at the temperamental level, and a man is expected to live very much in the 'here and now,' to be highly extraverted, and to give very free expression to his feelings.
>
> Whereas the Western child is early introduced to building blocks, keys in locks, water taps, and a multiplicity of items and events which constrain him to think in terms of spatiotemporal relations and mechanical causation, the African child receives instead an education which depends much more exclusively on the spoken word and which is relatively highly charged with drama and emotion.[184]

Carothers' research made two significant points: The first related to

---

183 McLuhan Marshall. *Understanding Media: The Extensions of Man*. MIT Press, London 1994, p. 60
184 See: McLuhan Marshall. *The Gutenberg Galaxy: The Making of Typographic Man*. University of Toronto Press, Canada 1962, p. 18

the social unit that speech provided. As overviewed above, intersubjective communication favored family and community ties considering the traditions, principles, and experiences of group members are communicated directly by word of mouth. He found that the individual could not separate from the community because that would entail not being able to develop nor learn their culture. In the case of westerners, born into a world with the written phonetic alphabet, Carothers argued they do not have a similar direct tie to their community. This is because literate learning does not necessarily stem from a subject. As discussed, written sources are objects that render education impersonal. This implies that humans no longer see themselves as a substantial part of a group, but instead, more likely to take notice of their individuality and orientation as autonomous beings.

On the other hand, some research has shown that illiterate groups may be more predisposed to expressing their feelings. It has been argued that this may be due to the fact that these groups are more exposed to interpersonal relationships on which they depend to develop over the life course. This implies that rationality is less developed, as the environment, orality, foments the development of other abilities, as we have already noted about Plato's critique of ancient Greece's educational method. Functionally, the phonetic alphabet also favors the development of the intellect; humans need to read what is presented to them and link it to a certain reality. These two actions are carried out continuously to understand what is being read, causing a reader to move away from reality to understand what a certain sign represents intellectually. For these reasons, Marshall McLuhan indicated that visual cultures were fragmented, while acoustic cultures were integrated. Meaning, he insisted that in oral-based learning communities functions of individuals are more closer aligned with reality than literate cultures. To him, this was catalyzed by the phonetic alphabet, that intensified and extended sight, reducing, and sometimes separating the role of other senses, such as sound, touch, and taste. Reinforcing this sentiment, Von Humboldt stated:

> The mental striving breaks out through the lips in language, the product of that striving returns back to the speaker's ear. Thus the idea becomes transformed into real objectivity, without being deprived of subjectivity on that account.[185]

In this sense, the Russian neuropsychologist Alexander Romanovich

---

185 Humboldt Von, Wilhelm. *On Language: On the Diversity of Human Language Construction and its Influence on the Mental Development of the Human Species.* Cambridge University Press, New York 1999, p. 56

Luria, the founder of Cultural-Historical Psychology and one of the leaders of the Vygotsky Circle, put forward that the area of the brain that controlled sequencing. Additionally, he believed that mathematical and scientific thought was conducted in the prefrontal region of the brain's left hemisphere, alleging that: "The mental process for writing a word entails still another specialization: Putting the letters in the proper sequence to form the word."[186] For him, the linear sequence implied a type of thought unique to the literate mind which required following a determined order of reading, resulting in lineal thought for purposes of accessing written information. Luria thought literate learning stimulated this brain part in any experience, including cultural ones. On the other hand, he found that the right hemisphere was predominant in illiterate folks; especially, regarding their capacity to emote, due to their social realtions, which centralized empathy and community. His research provided one understanding of how the written alphabet, with its linear structure, was able to create the conditions that led to the development of patriarchal Western logic, science, and technology.[187]

According to Marshall McLuhan, phonetic cultures granted humans tools to suppress their feelings and emotions. To him, acting without reacting or seeing oneself actively involved, was a peculiar advantage of the literate West, inclined by a detachment that literacy promoted. McLuhan stressed that the alphabet dissociated and abstracted images and sounds, separating meaning from letters' sounds, engendering words had no direct relation to the reality they were made to name.[188]

According to David Diringer, a British linguist, paleographer, and writer famous for his research regarding writing systems, the alphabet was a system that was universally used by civilized people, leading to detribalization. Said otherwise, he was concerned with how the system entailed a process of individualization vis-à-vis the community; when "civilized" human beings moved away from primary orality, they did also from social groups. Again, for Diringer, the phonetic alphabet individualized communities. He insisted that those without phonetic alphabets remained collective, for example, Chinese and Japanese cultures. These cultures do not use phonetic alphabets. They use ideograms to communicate, denoting an important difference in their communal perceptions of reality. In fact, the direct antecedent of any independent writing system known to man was a pictographic-ideographic

---

[186] McLuhan Marshall and Powers B. R. *The Global Village: Transformations in World Life and Media in the 21st Century*. Barcelona: Gedisa, 1989 p. 69 (In Spanish)

[187] Ibidem

[188] McLuhan Marshall. *The Gutenberg Galaxy: The Making of Typographic Man*. University of Toronto Press, Canada 1962, p. 47

stage, which derived its name from the signs used: pictograms and ideograms. A pictogram could be described as a separate sign, signifying a represented object. It is said that pictographic writing emerged through analysis and abstraction.

Ideograms are related to pictograms, and are signs that represent ideas, qualities, actions, and at times, objects, none of which can be directly represented by a pictogram. While pictograms are copies of nature, ideograms are new creations, stimulating an author's creative faculties.

While it is true that ideograms and pictograms were a form of language prior to phonetic writing organization, it is important to note that they each arose separately, regardless of language. And, in ancient times there was no link between these signs and the words they signified.

On the other hand, as a form of organization, phonetic writing is different because the signs represent sounds; each of the signs representing a vowel or consonant. Certain exceptions exist in some languages where two consonants can be joined. These are called double consonants, like the x in Greek, which equals the ks combination, and the ψ, which equals the ps combination. The leap towards a phonetic alphabet meant having to find signs for single consonants, entirely separating them from reality. On the flip side, spoken vowel sounds can exist by themselves—i.e. we can say a, e, i, etc.—but the consonant sounds cannot be used this way, as they need to be attached to a vowel to be pronounceable, for example, p = pe. However, consonants can be separated from the vowel in writing. The advantage of pictographic languages lies in that images attract the eye quickly and connect us directly to reality. Relatedly, there are some people who have a heightened visual memory that allows them to remember images more easily than words. Today we know the use of both simultaneously can be extremely useful for everyday learning. Likewise, visual dominant media seem to prefer depicting images to audiences. This may enable people to grasp what is being transmitted to them more efficiently imbedding in their memory. However, this method may not be advantageous to a rational human being's intellectual capacities.

Arguably the disadvantage of pictography was its inability to illustrate multiple concepts. Also, the meaning of a figure may be forgotten, and a person who has never seen such an image before, or has never been told what it represents, may find it challenging to interpret. For example, a cartoon appearing in a newspaper now might be easy for someone to interpret. But, a cartoon from a newspaper from fifteen years ago may not. Some cultures used to depend entirely on this medium to preserve their customs and traditions, which entailed (as the prior Grecian example) communicating knowledge to the next generations compellingly. The issue was—what happened if a bond was broken and there was no longer anyone who could pass down ancestral knowledge? Alfred Moorhouse illustrated one answer in *The Triumph of the Alphabet: A History of Writing*:

> According to tradition, the people of Easter Island used to gather once a year to hear the contents of their ancient pictographic wooden tablets. These tablets recorded the genealogy and legends of the land their ancestors migrated from. Their significance was limited to the native royal family and a few other individuals, among them the priests. In 1863, Peruvian slave traders arrived in the island and took with them all of the leaders; later, catholic missionaries arrived, and burned a great number of those tablets due to being of pagan origin. This resulted in no one being able to read those that were salvaged, and a great part of the indigenous culture was lost.[189]

As depicted above, it has been proposed that because of this many societies have lost their collective identity, instead adapting to new customs in accordance with new circumstances of each era. Tragically, during this process, individual, cultural, and sociohistorical traces have been lost.

The phonetic alphabet does not allow for the loss of prior dominant cultures to happen as easily because once the sign and its use are known, with the correct translation tools humans can decipher any remaining records. However, the alphabet rendered ancient pictograms indecipherable, functionally obsolescing the ability to interpret these other languages and cultures.

However, as has been detailed extensively throughout this study, this medium introduced taken for granted abstraction challenges; letters represent intangible things. Even in the process of learning a medium itself, we seek to relate it to some reality. For example, "A" is for "Apple," but the truth is that each letter of the alphabet does not represent anything alone. Each one is not even useful on its own—only when words are formed to be recognized, or ascribed a meaning. In any event, this type of language, if used correctly, has greater benefits than pictographic and even oral languages. Its use readily cultivates the human mind, even in solitude, which has not been done with any other type of language. Others required community membership to learn what was known, and in turn to transmit shared sense-making, unchanged, intact, and devoid of any progress.

Moreover, Marshall McLuhan insisted that printed ideograms were entirely different from typography based upon the phonetic alphabet. He said that was because the ideogram, moreso than the hieroglyph, was a complex

---

189   Moorhouse Alfred C. *Historia del alfabeto*. FCE, México 1982, p. 221 (In Spanish)

Gestalt involving engagement of all of the senses simultaneously. According to McLuhan, the ideogram did not afford any separation and specialization of sense, or any breaking apart of sight and sound and meaning, which was central to the phonetic alphabet.[190]

In this way, according to the research of a variety of authors that I have outlined thus far, and evidenced by the circumstances of the societies in which such effects manifest, Marshall McLuhan illustrated the importance of media as a formal cause of human development. His critique of the phonetic language related to the necessary abstraction process, which as demonstrated, lead humans to separate from their senses. Part and parcel, intelligence has apprehended signs without depending on direct relationship with reality. Concurrently, each symbol stopped representing anything but a sound. As such, literacy individualized humans, and lead them to naturalize a separation of themselves from surroundings. Arguably, this self-focus instilled an increasing disconnect from their environments. Marshall McLuhan did not have a clear position regarding this "detribalization". In several of his writings he claimed neutrality on this matter: "Whether such personal abstraction and social detribalization be a 'good thing' it's not for any individual to determine."[191] In other words, he seemed annoyed by the effects of the alphabet:

> It follows, of course, that literate man, when we met him in the Greek world, is a split man, a schizophrenic, as all literate men have been since the invention of the phonetic alphabet.[192]

Following the above idea that the alphabet caused a visual separation of sight, sound, and meaning, the social and psychological impacts of media were the fundamental foci of McLuhan's criticisms. As Rousseau (and later the romantic poets and philosophers) proclaimed long ago, the literate individual experienced a broad dissociation from their imaginative, emotional, and sensorial life. In this double-edged view, while the literate Westerner suffered from a significant dissociation from their inner sensibility when using the alphabet, they also attained personal freedom to move away from the clan and family unit.[193] That is why Marshall McLuhan repeated that the preliterate individual tended to be conservative, while the literate was likely more liberal.

In the case of Aristotle, he believed speech to be indispensable to the

---

190   McLuhan Marshall. *The Gutenberg Galaxy: The Making of Typographic Man.* University of Toronto Press, Canada 1962, p. 34-35
191   *Ibid*, p. 48
192   McLuhan Eric, Zingrone Frank. *Essential McLuhan.* Anansi, Toronto 1995, p. 117
193   McLuhan Marshall. *Understanding Media: the Extensions of Man.* MIT Press, London 1994, p. 100

development of a male human's intelligence, their *logos*; in his purview, the intersubjective relationship was a necessary condition for human accomplishment, but this did not necessarily imply an essential modification in the individual. In other words, to him, even if it was true that men changed as they thought, such change was only accidental since they remain humans through knowledge and did not transform into other entities by the fact that they contained more or less information. For Aristotle, language was an efficient cause of human improvement rather than a formal cause of change because, thanks to efficient cause, men could reach their ultimate goal: happiness via truth.

In summary, both Aristotle and Marshall McLuhan realized the value of speech compared to written language. Socrates dedicated much of his life to teaching through orality, language, and dialectics. For him, teaching should not take place in a closed space nor be based on something as impersonal as a book. Socrates stressed that true teaching took place intersubjectively, the only way men could "know themselves" and realize their lack of knowledge; only through social interaction could men reach perfection. Marshall McLuhan also cited the example of Christ, who was said not to teach via the phonetic alphabet because orality was essential for his advice to remain salient in the consciousnesses of men. To justify why Socrates and Christ, as teachers, did not link their teachings to Scripture, Marshall McLuhan quoted *Summa Theologica III, q. 42, a. 4:*

> I answer by saying that it is fitting that Christ did not commit his teaching to writing. First on account of his own dignity; for the more excellent the teacher, the more excellent is manner of teaching ought to be. And therefore, it was fitting that Christ, as the most excellent of teachers, should adopt that manner of teaching whereby his doctrine would be imprinted on the hearts of his hearers. For which reason it is said in Matthew vii, 29, that 'he was teaching them as one having power.' For which reason, even among the pagans Pythagoras and Socrates, who were most excellent teachers, did not want to write anything.[194]

Both were described as great teachers whose disciples were influenced by the media of their time period. To recap, in chronological order, we started with Plato, who saw merit in documenting lectures of his master in his *Dialogues*, which remain intact, despite passage of time.

Had it not been for these writings, the Socratic teachings likely would have

---

194   McLuhan Marshall. *The Gutenberg Galaxy: The Making of Typographic Man.* University of Toronto Press, Canada 1962, p. 98

been lost once the Greeks were conquered and their stories were adapted into Christian, Muslim, and/or Jewish worlds. As noted above, the challenge of oral teaching was that when knowledgeable people pass away, their teachings may die with them. It is not so with scripture; Christians must have understood this, evidenced by their dissemination of the word of Christ throughout the Roman territory and beyond. This became easier once the gospels, letters, and so forth were written; it became easier for their Master's word to reach everywhere without a need for them to be present.

As such, J. C. Carothers stated that it was only when the written, and especially, printed word appeared on the scene, that the stage was set for words to lose their magical powers and vulnerabilities.[195] As thoroughly discussed, it is said that orality's intersubjectivity oriented speakers towards consciousness. What could be learned from this lifestyle remains deeply engraved in the human being, who then acted accordingly to what they were taught. On the other hand, the written word allegedly inclined a loss of directly transmissible lessons because when words were written, they became part of the visual world. Functionally, the phonetic alphabet favors images over sounds, fixing our eyes on the text and interpretation of each symbol to capture information and gleam the message being sent. This implies that each subject must decipher a message through their experiences, not unlike a mosaic in which what is written is supplemented by the information already obtained, in order to garner a closer understanding of any written text.

Certain problems have arisen from this. First, the information captured is tinted with subjectivity because when we decipher messages through a lens of our own experiences, our interpretation inevitably makes impossible any claim to objectivity. The question is—what happens when interpreter's paraphrase and/or translate another text? For one, as this action is repeated over time, the transmitted message becomes altered, and charged with the subjectivity of each receiver. In this way, what the original author wished to convey could become completely lost. Secondly, another problematic effect is that interpretation will vary based on what can be seen by any one translator. Said otherwise, as a medium, orality ensured humans retained a sense of belonging to community in pursuit of the common good. According to aforementioned theorists, this method allegedly resulted in teachings being transmitted more authentically by teachers. In comparison, it has been said that tthe phonetic alphabet emphasized visual symbols and imagery, which theorists like McLuhan argued lead humans to be more concerned about appearances, conformity, and respectability. Little by little, humanity became uniform and homogeneous, a sense of community

---

195 McLuhan Marshall. *The Gutenberg Galaxy: The Making of Typographic Man*. University of Toronto Press, Canada 1962, p. 19

was lost, and the individual became our focal point. Carothers explained this:

> When words are written, they become, of course, a part of the visual world. Like most of the elements of the visual world, they become static things and lose, as such, the dynamism which is so characteristic of the auditory world in general, and of the spoken word in particular. They lose much of the personal element, in the sense that the heard word is most commonly directed at oneself, whereas the seen word most commonly is not, and can be read or not as whim dictates. (...) Thus, in general, words, by becoming visible, join a world of relative indifference to the viewer—a world from which the magic 'power' of the words has been abstracted.[196]

As he elucidated, each medium of communication oriented its own transmission problems. Each one in some way modified the information being sent, as well as how it will be received by a recipient. For Marshall McLuhan, this separation of the senses which, at times, detached humans even from their own rationality was most important. Technology and media extended one sense more than another, numbing other human perceptions, in order for the information to get through.

Contemporary Media and Their Influence on Humans

In contemporary times, some media may appear as if not to have an influence on us, but they do, without a doubt. Referring to media prior to and of his own lifetime, Marshall McLuhan extensively traced out the transformative power of electric light which illuminated human abilities to capture more information. For example, the experience of watching a game at night time was upgraded through the introduction of light, ensuring the team could play adequately, and the viewers could better observe what was happening. Another enlightening example that, the medium is the message. McLuhan wrote extensively on how when lights are turned on, a world of sense, appears, only to then disappear again when they are turned back off.[197] Without it, we would likely remain more inactive indoors at night. The mass introduction of electric light also sparked the insurgence of other media to develop, like transport. McLuhan

---

196 McLuhan Marshall. *The Gutenberg Galaxy: The Making of Typographic Man*. University of Toronto Press, Canada 1962, p. 20
197 McLuhan Marshall. *Understanding Media: the Extensions of Man*. MIT Press, London 1994, p. 144

argued these media could be seen as communication as well, because they revolutionized human abilities to reach places never conceivable before that. In his eyes, each of these new media also carried information. Specifically, he said, "Each form of transport not only carries, but translates and transforms the sender, the receiver, and the message."[198] For instance, vehicles changed human perception because, through speed, it increased our power to develop anywhere. These extensions also transformed the formation of other societal groups, also thanks to the newfound ability to move swiftly from one place to another. Infrastructurally, transportation could also be associated with decentralization because human beings no longer had to be in one location. They could move around locale, separating themselves from the community, while strengthening their individuality and ego.

The increased efficiency of transportation and communications additionally divided people, now less tied to specific areas. In addition, this inspired reflection and comprehension of limits and threats to the ego; therefore, some humans tried to avoid them. Hence why Nietzsche said that, "understanding stops action, and men of action seem to have an intuition of the fact in their shunning the dangers of comprehension."[199] Speed lead others to lose themselves, as they had no time to center themselves. On the topic of this chaotic shift, Marshall McLuhan proclaimed:

> Our speed-up today is not a slow explosion outward from center to margins but an instant implosion and an interfusion of space and functions.[200]

Said otherwise, according to him, cars, trains, and all other vehicles used for transportation were actually not the central mechanism when referring to impactful physical media. He argued that the more significant media were actually those created for them: roads, factories, gas stations, and all else that emerge as a consequence of transport. Furthermore, these transformed the mobility of our lives generating even more acceleration and new perceptive realities. As a reminder, McLuhan was convinced transformation occurred in the *logos;* in individual minds, which were affected by dominant mediums. Thus, some probing questions might be: who are affected by media? If all aforementioned findings hold true, the answer is—everyone because, whether we use transport or any other media, regardless of overt acceptance, we cannot avoid living in societies "with" them. For these reasons, even unwittingly, we

---

198 *Ibid,* p. 102
199 *Idem*
200 *Ibid* p. 106

are considerably affected by these extensions. Our lives and ways of thinking would not be the same without them. Hence, for Marshall McLuhan, media were societal and individual formal causes because the changes they generated were not accidental; they directly affected and were essential to our cognition, sense-making, and actions. To provide an example, we would not be able to even think about a vacation to Europe if we did not have ways to travel there. Similarly, we would not be able to analyze a modern author's thinking if their work did not exist. This leads back to the phonetic alphabet—the first medium that was argued to have split our senses, fragmenting our being. With it came numerals, extending our sight as the crucial sense for their development. And according to McLuhan's analysis, numbers, not numerals, extended our sense of touch, further revolutionizing another primary means through which we grasp reality. Other authors have also remarked on the primacy of touch as a unifier of all the other senses extending the brain. This is because the skin, as a communication organ, is extremely complex and versatile, and has multiple functions related to the entire body. This relationship is channeled through the nervous system, in which heat and/or cold are also perceived, all over our entire bodily surfaces. Ergo, Marshall McLuhan proposed:

> Clothing and housing, as extensions of skin and heat-control mechanisms, are media of communication, first of all, in the sense that they shape and rearrange the patterns of human association and community.[201]

McLuhan felt the skin was a vital human organ that spurred developed of additional media of communication for its protection. At the same time, clothing and housing also birthed other changes in the individual and in society; extensions of our sense of touch generated both security and insecurity, fear and courage, and many more. These inventions further extended the entire body, some of which stimulated acceleration of blood circulation, also influenced by contact with another person. Likewise, a person who experiences fear or pain might regain physiological balance through tactile contact with another person, providing comfort. McLuhan suggested this function was set aside by numerals. He connected these phenomena being that numerals were visual, influencing an increased reliance on sight and a concurrent decrease in touch. Another source who made this connection was László Moholy-Nagy, a 19th-century Hungarian painter, photographer, and Bauhaus teacher. As a multimodal artist, Moholy-Nagy was heavily influenced by constructivism, and

---

201 McLuhan Marshall. *Understanding Media: the Extensions of Man*. MIT Press, London 1994, p. 57

advocated the integration of technology and industry into the arts, noticing that from his European perspective, the United States seemed to be the land of abstractions where numbers appeared to have taken on an existence of their own. His support for this was the importance given to numbers by U.S. cultural institutions and industries. For example, saying "90-60-90" or "36-24-36" would describe something as concrete and universal, in turn linking it to tactility; he believed these numbers described proportions of an ideal feminine form.[202] In the Western world, capitalists quantified measurements normalized an ideological and material association of time with money. As discussed, this mindset has origins in literacy, since numbers only have meaning for individuals exposed to writing and reading. So, for preliterate folks, numbers had no use; their lives were structured around direct connections, not symbolic abstracts.

Even current technologies utilize binary adapted number systems in order to operate. Can we further evolve the phonetic alphabet, attaining utopian universal communication, without unpacking the dehumanizing realities that claims to objectivity and mathematic languages caused?

As theorists have documented, numbers caused measurements of reality in various ways: to predict economic events, generate beauty patterns, track movements, etc.. Time is another medium that revolutionized our covert and overt actions in ways that, especially in the late-stage neoliberal capitalist context, pervade into every sphere of our lives. Time talks. (...) It can shout the truth where words lie."[203] Time communicates things that words do not, either because they are unknown or do not want to be said. It is said that actions speak louder than words. Actions can say a lot more about who we are than what we say because we can use words to hide what we feel or think. Literate individuals also have the capacity to split their being into two—what they think and what they say. Likewise, time is a communicator of realities, despite its naturalized presence.

Time has enormous influence on humans and the need to know this can be illustrated with examples of how one's sense of time is experienced differently in different cultures. For instance, imagine a U.S. farmer is given a job in a Latin American country. They agree to meet their new boss at a specific time to talk about the terms of employment and related expectations. The day arrives, and the employee arrives at their new office ten minutes early. The secretary welcomes them graciously and suggests they take a seat until the boss arrives. Ten, fifteen, twenty minutes pass. The employee asks the secretary to call the boss—perhaps they forgot about the meeting. The secretary replies that they need not worry since the boss knows of the meeting. This response is met with

---

202 *Ibid* p. 57
203 Hall T. Edward. *The Silent Language*. Anchor Books, New York 1959, p. 1

anger, given the delay. After waiting for one hour, the annoyed employee leaves the office, feeling they were disrespected by the company's boss who kept them waiting for so long.

This case study exemplified a possible culture clash and transgression because different cultural expressions and relationships with time have been normalized in different continental regions. We see here, for North Americans, punctuality is very important. To them, promptness is a sign of respect and recognition of another person's importance. Someone born here is socialized into arriving ahead of time to ensure the meeting is conducted efficiently, and so as not to disrespect the other. In Latin American countries, time is thought of differently. In these environments, when people agree on a time to meet, it may mean arriving twenty, thirty, or sixty minutes late. Furthermore, when someone invites guests to a party, the organizers expect their guests to arrive at least an hour after the time they indicated. This is not considered disrespectful to the host; it is simply the custom in places where, as we can see, time is perceived differently.

Difficulties arise when people do not realize that they are being subjected to different ways of communication when they move to another country. Some of these ways of being circulate around language and time, and others refer to the relationships with time. Messages transmitted in one society suppress taken for granted elements of others, possibly generating culture shock. It seems that: "The thought of what is being communicated is what hurts."[204] Said more directly, as a result of being born into a certain time-based culture, people interpret signs in different ways, and if people do not know communication may suffer because these "media" could be perceived ambiguously. Any one environment is a medium in itself, containing messages devoid of formalities of speech or written language. Some communicology experts refer to this as acoustic space:

> Acoustic space is a dynamic or harmonic field. It exists while the music or sound persists. And the hearer is one with it, as with music. Acoustic space is the space-world of the primeval man.[205]

One could argue this space was more evident for tribal societies because their overriding sense was hearing. As has been discussed, literate humans separated from hearing and focused on sight. The process of this transition oriented them to lose sight of media, as central as time, in the acoustic space. One might say that time has a subjective connotation: even among people

---

204   Hall T. Edward, *The Silent Language*. Anchor Books, New York 1959, p. 6
205   McLuhan Marshall. *Counter-blast*. Harcourt, New York 1969, p. 79

from the same place. In Mexico, we commonly use the phrase: "*Tú tiempo o el mío*" ("your time or mine"). For some Indigenous people, time has an entirely different value than for North Americans. Events, parties, and celebrations begin when the time arrives and not before. "What would you think of a people who had no word for time? My people have no word for "late" or for "waiting" for that matter."[206] For example, once a foreigner arrived to a village to observe how they celebrated a special occasion. Beforehand, they asked locals what time the celebrations begin. They replied: "When the time comes." The American failed to understand this phrase at first, so they repeated their question. The annoyed Indigenous people explained that there was no exact time scheduled, and that they would simply begin when the time came. This left the foreigner surprised. They asked how they would know it was starting, to which locals replied: "When the drums begin to sound." And so, it happened. Late at night, the drums began sounding, announcing that the time had come.

As we can see from these two examples, time is an "essential" part of human development. Often, cultural matters determine an individuals' acts and thoughts. If we consider the social environment and society holistically, we could say that the medium is indeed formal cause of change in the individual since it absolutely determines both the environment and the people wthin it. On the other hand, if we consider the elements separately: humans, society, and medium—the media of communication turn out to be efficient causes of change in societies, since they are external causes that move or condition the humans , and thus, society, to act one way or another.

Finally, I will touch upon the subject of the image as a medium of communication and transformer of society since it has been present throughout human history and has generated communication through various extensions. Even though I shall not delve into the history of the image, I do refer to photography as a model from which antiquity and modernity emerged.

In ancient Greece, Plato sharply criticized artists for the way they presented their works. We saw this when we discussed the subject of speech. For Plato, images, sculptures, and poetry were no more than crude imitations of what was real. Therefore, he considered artistic productions unhelpful mediums for the *Republic,* if not regulated and directed towards the common good.

In this regard, it must be said that art has never pretended to be "reality," as no image is like reality. The artist takes some aspects. capturing in matter, and thereby expressing their feelings. Images are based on speech, as much as written language conventions, and are signs that represent something and, in turn, are interpreted by individuals. Nowadays, art and images are an extremely

---

206 Hall T. Edward. *The Silent Language*, Anchor Books, New York 1959, p. 13

important resource for the entertainment industry, since we live in an age where we are moved towards a specific end through illusions. This is where the importance of the image lies.

Marshall McLuhan provided an example of how this medium has been used in society:

> Recently an imaginative school principal in a slum area provided each student in the school with a photograph of himself. The classrooms of the school were abundantly supplied with large mirrors. The result was an astounding increase in the learning rate. The slum child has ordinarily very little visual orientation. He does not see himself as becoming something. He does not envisage distant goals and objectives. He is deeply involved in his own world from day to day, and can establish no beachhead in the highly specialized sense life of visual man. The plight of the slum child, via the TV image, is increasingly extended to the entire population.[207]

The above example revealed, yet again, that "the medium is the message." When one presents a child with an image of themselves, the photograph itself, already sends a message that they are defined in a certain way. In the representation they can see themselves as a model. As a mediated process, some have argued photography provides an objective view of what exists, that subjects may otherwise be in denial about. It shows faults, qualities, and one clear perspective of what captured subjected and/or objects can be seen as, without failing to be a copy of reality. But, as a medium, it can also provide the individual with sufficient details to move forward, as in the example cited by Marshall McLuhan. He said photography created a, "museums without walls,"[208] affording worldly knowledge without needing to leave our home, contemplation of our or others joy, lamentations on suffering, etc.; to him, photography, as a medium, was an additional language abstracting realistic qualities that are captured on paper to be remembered, lived, and understood.

In this way, he insisted images were capable of capturing isolated moments in time in order to be preserved and relived in the future. Through use of a camera, he thought oone could see others from a higher perspective, functionally objectifying those who are photographed. McLuhan observed that from a photographer's perspective, certain aspects of a person are given importance; a part of them was abstracted and shown in the picture. In photographs, movie

---

207 McLuhan Marshall. *Understanding Media: the Extensions of Man*. MIT Press, London 1994, p. 142
208 *Ibid*

stars and pop idols enter public domain and are transformed into dreams money can buy. According to Marshall McLuhan, "They can be bought and hugged and thumbed more easily than public prostitutes."

> Jean Genet's The Balcony[209] is a play on this theme of society as a brothel environed by violence and horror. The avid desire of mankind to prostitute itself stands up against the chaos of revolution. The brothel remains firm and permanent amidst the most furious changes. In a word, photography has inspired Genet with the theme of the world since photography as a Brothel-without-Walls.[210]

In a certain tangible sense, with this medium, we can stop and observe reality in a permanent past, objectifying a moment reflecting the outside world. The process of producing visual images can be repeated as many times as we wish. In this sense, "the camera does not lie" because it only depict what it captures from reality; functionally, photography is writing with light, and it copies what the lens reveals to it, devoid of additional interpretation. Photography obsolesced painting, which, as a prior medium, also replicated a painter's chosen image of reality. Painting slightly differs from photography; however, creativity in the latter is often based upon impressionism and abstract art of the former. Likewise, thanks to photography, the press, cinema, and radio, a writer no longer needed to describe objects or events from reality; we are able to see what has happened. In this way, art was transformed from an external to internal construction.[211]

McLuhan argued photography was an intensified extension of humans visual capacity, numbing other senses. To him, the printed image had little to do with the semantic universe and nothing to do with the phonetic alphabet. He thought that the latter enabled us to think and translate what we are told,

---

209   *The Balcony* is a theatre piece by the French playwright Jean Genet published in 1956. The story takes place in an unnamed city suffering havoc from a revolution. *The Balcony* is the name of a brothel or a *House of Illusions* frequented by regular individuals to realize their fantasies. In that repertory of fantasies are those representing the clergy, the military establishment, and finally, the representative of the law. Thus, a microcosm is created among the representatives of the establishment inside a brothel while outside the revolution is mounting. According to some, this work shows the conflict between revolution and counterrevolution, and on a more philosophical level, the conflict between identity and illusion. A mechanism of meta-theater or theater within theater develops, resulting in great interest in the analysis of the piece. The scene unfolds; within the brothel, the illusions of the characters are represented and observed by the *Madame* and other characters.
210   McLuhan Marshall. *Understanding Media: the Extensions of Man*. MIT Press, London 1994, p. 210
211   *Ibid* p. 150

according to what was depicted, but that images did not need any kind of interpretation. McLuhan claimed whatever was being represented in an image was openly visible.

> Perhaps that is the readiest way to grasp the meaning of the photograph in creating a world of accelerated transience (...) Fashion is not a way of being informed or aware, but a way of being with it.[212]

Major changes occurred as a result of this medium. Marshall McLuhan argued it even reversed the purpose of travel, permitting once foreign and/or unknown encounters. It was no longer necessary for one to spend time traveling to far away places; instead, we could now access countless photographs that visually characterize a place, without ever needing to be there. Thus, travel agencies' slogans, like "Go Now, Pay Later," may as well say, "Go Now, Arrive Later."[213]

Ever since this invention, tourists arriving at the Leaning Tower of Pisa or to Arizona's Grand Canyon need only check their reactions to any monument long familiar to them, rather than taking photos[214] from their own perspective, emphasizing whatever appeared most meaningful to them. In a moment, anyone with a camera can capture a realistic scene that they could then keep the rest of their lives. Despite the fact this medium, and related others, may seem simply visual, like writing, Marshall McLuhan indicated that, "Electricity is only incidentally visual and auditory; it is primarily tactile."[215] This is because, upon closer examination, what is amplified by them is not only stored visuals that provoke memories, but also feelings, of that moment. Plus, photography would not have been possible without electricity, which, as we have seen, caused several changes in society, and the individual. However, interestingly, it seems that with the speed of electricity, our lives were also expedited; slowly, societies were woken up from an abundance of spare time, and the lethargy of their calmly performed activities. These changes spurred reflections on what and how things are done. Today, as a result of electric advances in technology, actions are immediate. Prophetically, McLuhan wrote of a kind of electric central nervous system:

> By electricity, we everywhere resume person-to-person relations as if on the smallest village scale. (...) The organic everywhere supplants the

---

212   *Ibid* p. 217
213   *Ibid* p. 219
214   *Idem*
215   *Ibid* p. 274

mechanical.[216]

Technologically, it could be argued that humans have reached a speed and velocity they are unprepared to handle. Considering the consequences of these mediated social and individual transformations, it seems the human being was not made to live at the speed of light. From being exposed to seemingly endless amounts of visual information and new media, humans could implode. The ubiquitous exposure to global information, at a tremendous speed could have arguably dangerous, extreme, and untold cognitive results. These media might be further dissociating our focus on visual and tactile phenomena; an entire society of electronically amplified, and thus, disembodied people moves more efficiently, yet these extensions might cost them any sense of personal identity. This is because, as overviewed in a prior section, electronic perceptions are not linked to any locale,[217] catalyzing losses of individual identity and community.

---

216 *Ibid* p. 282
217 McLuhan Marshall and Powers B. R. *The Global Village: Transformations in World Life and Media in the 21st Century*. Barcelona: Gedisa, 1989 p. 103 (In Spanish)

Marshall McLuhan's Formal Cause Is, in Fact, Aristotle's Efficient Cause

Throughout this study, we analyzed historical elements and media of communication, particularly speech, written language, and electricity, as well as transport, photography, and time—demonstrating how each acted as a kind of language, which changed socials relations and human development. This analysis was based upon the concept of formal cause and its relation to two authors: Aristotle and Marshall McLuhan, to better understand media theory from a philosophical perspective, and thus, achieve true interdisciplinarity between communication and philosophy.

In this section, I intend to conclude this discussion by comparing both authors' notions of formal cause and determine whether or not one can describe that media as formal cause. According to Marshall McLuhan, his media theory coincided with an Aristotelian notion of formal cause as the essence of being. Lastly, I conclude by distinguishing boundaries of each author's perspective.

Formal Cause as Intrinsic v. Efficient Cause as Extrinsic to the Being

Aristotle was the starting point for this analysis due to his precedence and his theory of four causes, which served as the basis for further discussion. This chapter will focus on a comparison of both authors' formal cause following a brief record of their approaches, given that an exhaustive examination of this topic has already been carried out in previous chapters.

As we have seen, Aristotelian causal thought centered on four main causes: material, formal, efficient, and final, as the basis for the understanding of reality, whichever it may be. To recap, matter referred to what a thing being examined was formed from, for example, bronze in the case of a statue, and humans and cooperation in the case of societies. Viewed separately and without a formal setting, this cause was identifiable as the substrate of change, meaning the aspect where change takes place. To Aristotle, matter, alone, was not reality in itself, or a being, as such, because it lacked form, which gave a thing its essence.

Lastly, and as he alleged in his writings on metaphysics, matter without form would be pure potential, a kind of non-being.

Secondly was formal cause, which in Aristotelian terms was the most important of all causes since it was the one that, based on language, showed the essence of things, and thus, their efficient and final cause. According to this, form determined matter and gave an actual entity to that which was mere potential or a possibility. To understand this cause better, one must distinguish between two elements a thing contained; one was accidents which, according to their definition, depended on a being, comprised of matter and form. An example might be a statue's color. Whether black or white, color does not exist alone; it must exist on a surface. Also, to him, as this element was "accidental," it did not affect a statue's essence. Meaning, statues would not cease to be if/when their color changed. In the case of societies, which have been defined as groups of people, further comprising distinct units of individuals who aims to cooperate and reach mutual fulfillment of life's purposes.[218] In these instances, accidents might be language, or skin color, to name a few. Aristotle proposed that none of these modified, in essence, what a society "was".

On the other hand, he said a hylomorphic being had substance. This type of being was defined as what it was by itself, not requiring another in order to exist. Instead, hylomorphic beings demonstrated that their entity as greater than, and unlike, that of accidents, since they was independent of any substrate. Moreover, in this view, substance was directly linked to form because it was what gave a thing its essence, making it what it was. In the example of a statue, substance would be the sculptural work, imitating nature. It would not need a certain color or a specific size to exist because it existed in and of itself. In the case of societies, substance would be the grouping of individuals for some purpose, regardless of any one person's particular characteristics or place of origin. In other words, a definition's content stated the essence of a thing. Thus, its substance, was what mattered. Any change in essence would modify a thing's definition, and thus, entirely changing the being.

Based on the above, one can see that in an Aristotelian view, substance, or essence, needed matter. For example, the bronze statue implied matter, "bronze," as well as form, determining it as a statue. Formal cause "needed" certain elements contained in a statue's material cause. The case of societies was much clearer, for there could be no goal-oriented groupings without individuals. Thus, both material and formal cause were necessary to a being, meaning they were intrinsic to it.

Thirdly, we have efficient cause, defined as that from which a primary source of change or rest derived. To Aristotle, this was what moved a statue

---

218   See Web. June 26, 2013 http://lema.rae.es/drae/?val=sociedad

to be one, and not anything else, e.g., a sculptor. Bronze was not naturally disposed towards becoming a work of art; the exertion that a human imposed on its matter was what lead it to conform as such. As was detailed above, this kind of cause had more to do with extrinsic aspects of a being, unlike formal cause was an intrinsic determination. In the case of societies, its efficient cause could be leaders or all that modified the movement of its actions. According to Aristotle, these were extrinsic to it. And as described, several categories were found to construct this kind of cause. In brief:

1) Perfective. The one which had to do with "artificial perfection," where a being's nature was not naturally predisposed for it, but an external agent leading it down such a path.

2) Preparative. Having to do with the disposition of a being's matter, becoming only that which its nature allowed. For example, in the case of bronze, its matter allowed it to become a statue, a column, a coin, but prevented it from becoming other things.

3) Contributory. That which did not operate for its own purpose but for the purpose of another. It accompanied the natural purpose determining a being to be what it was, so it may reach an artificial end. In the case of bronze, its natural purpose was being a metallic body that resulted from the amalgamation of copper and tin, sometimes with added zinc or some other material, allowing it to become something different from its nature, but originating from the same form. Theoretically, the difference between contributory and preparative was the basis of change; the former had to do with something's natural end and the latter with the disposition of matter that allowed for molding a thing towards something else.

4) Conceiving. This efficient cause related to an agent that transformed matter. An example of this kind of cause would be if a sculptor had an image of the sculpture of "David" in their mind and moved the marble to obtain that form.

Returning to Aristotle, fourth and last was final cause, which had to do with the purpose or reason towards which a being was aimed. Accordingly, this kind of cause was closely related to formal cause because a being's purpose oriented its determination. For example, in the case of societies, they were allegedly directed towards common good. Thus, each part of societies was aimed towards that end, their form determining them as such.

So, what kind of entity do media of communication have? Based on this analysis, how might we consider media in relation to societies or individuals? With all prior research in mind, if we focus on "mediums" as entities, we might distinguish each media by their causes; firstly, their material cause would be that of which they were made; this would vary by medium in question. As Marshall McLuhan did, I use language as a paradigm, being that this study was based upon his media premise. And, in his view, extensively reviewed herein, every medium was a new language.

Thus, each new media's material cause would be words, and the grammatical order that enabled them to be articulated in formation of its particular idea. A media's formal cause would be the system of symbols that comprised its essence. Without the internal order it possessed and its symbology, it would not constitute a language. This breakdown shows how material cause and formal cause are closely linked, given that without matter, essence would be lost.

Following this line of thought, the individual articulating symbols to form words, and thus, language, would be the medium's efficient cause. Using Aquinas's terminology, this might be contributive or conceiving, since both had to do with an agent's purpose, which went hand in hand with a natural aim. If we were to ask ourselves: which of the four causes would be the most important part of this language? The answer again would be that formal cause was because it was the aspect that, from an Aristotelian perspective, allegedly gave a being its essence, determining its matter, or configuring it to be what it was. Language's form would be more important than what it contained, meaning words and symbols. Likewise, returning to McLuhan's hypothesis that "the medium is the message," we could say that he took an Aristotelian approach to media in contemporary times, since he argued, the medium, form, determined matter, transmitting content.

However, it seemed that Marshall McLuhan was not only interested in the medium itself, but also changes in its historical, cultural, organizational, and moral relationships of individuals and societies, that he elaborately insisted also coincided with changes in media of communication. Therefore, Marshall McLuhan saw media not as tools used in different ways, but as part of our environment(s). In every situation we find ourselves, we encounter the influences of a medium.

Letter addressed from Marshall McLuhan to Jacques Maritain:

> I am quite aware that nobody has attempted to understand metamorphosis and causality in social institutions through a minute inspection of the sensory and perceptual changes resulting from the new environments. Surely the history of philosophy can never be

written without a complete awareness of these matters.

To which Maritain replied:

> I am overall agreement with what you have written to me... This, in its way, plays an essential role, which you insist on with good reason. But it does not account for everything. For, there is also formal causality, and I fear that you have not taken sufficient account of its role.[219]

This correspondance was key to Marshall McLuhan's argument regarding the medium and societies undergoing perpetual changes. To determine the media's place individually and socially, there is much to be gained from analyzing this relationship, also utilizing Aristotle's four causes.

We should note that for Marshall McLuhan, media were parts of society. As extensions of our extremities, and thus, tools for everything we did, they were an important part of each individual's development vis-à-vis society: "Any extension [...] whether of skin, hand, or foot, affects the whole physic and social complex."[220] To him, without them, without the different kinds of language, any organization such as communities would be practically impossible. Based on the above, one might say that societies material causes were the individuals, organizations, and medias used for communication. Formal cause would be the orderly grouping of individuals, via their media, towards a shared end. If this is correct, media would always exist in societies. They may vary in type, but that would be irrelevant because they would not modify the direction of societal changes. Likewise, from this perspective, when a being changes in form, it stops "being what it was" in order to become something different. This is not the case regarding the function of media; they do not modify the essence of either societies or individuals.

Structurally, societies' efficient causes could be said to be rulers and media of communication because, within societies, they have power to modify ways aims are achieved, even diverting from the common good towards other goals. Keeping in mind, from an Aristotelian point of view, efficient cause elicits an extrinsic movement from beings, leading them towards a certain direction,

---

[219] A letter addressed to Jacques Maritain from May 28, 1969, which is unpublished. See: McLuhan Marshall, McLuhan Eric. *Media and Formal Cause*. NeoPoiesis Press, Texas 2011, p. 4. Together with Étienne Gilson, Jacques Maritain carried out research and taught for some time at the Pontifical Institute for Medieval Studies, which was located at a short distance from Marshall McLuhan's office at the St. Michael's College campus. According to the latter's son, Eric McLuhan, their conversations were frequent.

[220] McLuhan Marshall, McLuhan Eric. *Media and Formal Cause*. NeoPoiesis Press, Texas 2011, p. 2

according to their form. And, according to Marshall McLuhan, this was the case of media; as humans, we are "conditioned" by our environment(s) and our media. Everything we come in contact with immediately becomes a condition of our existence, be it family, institutions to which we belong (or not), our friends, and the media that permeates our social relations. If these two theorists were correct, the human being is a conditioned being, therefore directed by media:

> The new medium of TV as an environment creates new occupations. (...) But the effects of TV on the movie go unnoticed, and the effects of the TV environment in altering the entire character of human sensibility and sensory ratios is completely ignored.[221]

However, one might say humans do not cease to exist as human beings because of media; they merely orient us in one direction to another. These human extensions are an extrinsic cause, an efficient cause for our behaviors in societies.

Marshall McLuhan insisted that a medium's content was of the least importance in communication since what truly impacted a person was the medium through which a message was conveyed. Therefore, I agree with his assertion that a message's form determines the matter it contains, i.e., the information being sent. Thus, the medium is a formal cause, the essence of a relationship between the content and its container. However, I argue this kind of causality does not apply to the relationship between the media and societies, which we would deem as efficient causalities that lead humans to behave in certain ways. According to McLuhan, media changed human rationality because their characteristics forced human beings to intensify some of our senses over others, changing our lifestyles. This inclined humans to act certain ways. For example, it was said that, due to the introduction of speech, humans were then able to understand information consciously or unconsciously. The ear mediated human information directly and allowed them to listen to their surroundings. Therefore, McLuhan, and others, reported that the tribal or acoustic human was concerned with their environment(s). Once literacy was introduced, they agreed that was no longer the case. They argued that literate people who obtained information through use of the phonetic alphabet, visualized words; first, to read, and then, to interpret what they were perceiving. Allegedly, due to this split in the information caused by writing, the individual was divided between what was learned and what was in their consciousness. For these reasons, media theorists of this variety, proposed that literate humans

---

221 *Idem*

came to see the world through concepts, while intensifying their visual sense, so that they can focus only on certain things. Therefore, they were more interested in only one part of reality, lacking a direct access that tribal humans had. Thus, they disengaged from their environment(s) and focused in on themselves. That was why Marshall McLuhan asserted that, "Visual culture is fragmented; acoustic culture is integrated."[222]

That which "lead" the individual to behave in different ways was, of course, the communication medium, used in order to relate with others, or with the world. One could also say this implies that the environment was human behavior's efficient cause and not its formal cause. Said otherwise, a being's formal cause would lead it to be, in essence, something different, and as we have seen, humans did not cease to be humans under a medium's influence; on the contrary, they continued being human, but their behavior was modified by the tools they used, which were external. In addition, formal cause is intrinsic to humans, while the vessels that humans "use" are extrinsic. We may, therefore, conclude that, in a sense, mediums are a formal cause, as they determine our content; "the medium is the message," and in a different sense, change's efficient cause, since they condition human beings, but do not determine them the way formal cause would.

---

222 McLuhan Marshall and Powers B. R. *The Global Village: Transformations in World Life and Media in the 21st Century*. Barcelona: Gedisa, 1989 p. 31 (In Spanish)

Conclusions

When it came to media of communication, Marshall McLuhan was a revolutionary of his time. It is not by chance that he is still considered today to be an authority on these subjects. In his work, he showed how societies have changed over time, depending on the media of communication of each age. Primarily, through the use of speech. From birth, humans listen to sounds of nature, their surroundings, and peers. As some aforementioned theorists have detailed, we are placed in the midst of an acoustic world from which we have to learn and imitate to survive. Later phonetic language was created, writing, and with it came a complete change in how reality was perceived; the alphabet emphasized the eye over the ear. Cognizant subjects concentrated more on what they saw and not on what they heard. It was unlikely for people to perceive an environment they were immersed within; instead, many observed isolated events. We moved from one word to the next, from one line to another, and in this way, we "read the environment" as if it were a book. New media have been created, subsequently, always based on language, which according to Marshall McLuhan, have been the foundation of our development since its creation.

Thus, McLuhan focused on a study of media to better understand the changes they caused in the individual. According to Lance Strate, "Marshall McLuhan explained media, and his explanation, his media ecology, also explained McLuhan."[223] It could be said that he set out to study media and society, but focused on what was produced through the relationships between them; that space that the medium creates, and is shaped, in a way that affects subjects in multiple ways, leading to further developments in societies and/or vice versa.

Long before the digital age, Marshall McLuhan understood media, including the medium and mediation, as opposing concepts. Hence his classic aphorism of "the medium is the message," which was the basis of this study. With it, he developed a thesis contrary to many theorists of his time's common sense and belief. In fact, this was the basis for understanding his aphorism. Arugably, the phrase would not have had the impact it did without understanding what the medium and the content were, without understanding

---

223 Strate L., Wachtel E. *The Legacy of McLuhan*. Hampton Press, Inc. New Jersey, 2005, p. 27

that what is contradictory is common, that the message is the medium.

The phrase was a call to action to pay attention to what remained hidden from our senses and, therefore, fundamentally changes our understanding of the world. Medium shape the way we communicate, think, perceive, and organize ourselves. According to Strate, Marshall McLuhan's approach to media was materialist and based on an analysis of the physical environment—artifacts and technologies—in addition to the human body and its extensions. However, unlike Karl Marx's dialectical materialism, Marshall McLuhan provided a grammatical and rhetorical one[224] since he realized the importance of these effects, produced by media, that impacted the essence of an individual and, thus, societies. While it is true that the message comes from a medium, the configuration of mediums determine the way in which a message reaches us, for it gives "form" to the information being sent to the matter contained therein. Thus, it could be concluded that form determines matter, and here lies the link to Aristotle and his theory of the four causes.

The medium can then be seen as a crux of change, the essence of history, yet, has remained hidden from human eyes because our attentions have always focused more on matter than form.

For Marshall McLuhan, the medium had to do not only with what was material but also with the ways, modes, and methods through which humans operated in the material world. "The medium is the message" perfectly expressed the notion of how one did something, and had much to do with the results obtained, regardless of one's initial intent. This relates to the old sayings, "Ask a stupid question and you'll get a stupid answer" and "You've made your bed, now lie in it."

We have also determined that the medium may be analyzed via a philosophical perspective, suggested by Marshall McLuhan himself, and referring to formal cause. I highlighted McLuhan's approach in this study, in conversation with Aristotle, the father of the four causes theory, as the combination allowed for a developed analysis of communication from a philosophical point of view to further enhance the understanding of those with a greater knowledge of philosophy rather than communication. As has been shown throughout, media condition the way individuals act and think. Examining speech examples reveals that this is fundamental to human life. With the introduction of languages, our thought processes changed. We cannot think without speech. When we refer to a real object, we immediately use the "medium" in order to talk about it. The only reference we have is the "medium," not reality, as the latter manifests itself through naming practices. These labels engender particular versions of reality, growing cognitively. Language allowed

---

224   *Ibid*, p.28

us to develop as humans because only through others can we know who we are and perfect ourselves through relationships. However, one problem that speech caused was the need to always have someone who could transmit knowledge to someone else. Intersubjectivity with certain individuals was necessary, if one wanted to preserve continuity in teachings and customs, ensuring that information did not change; otherwise, the customs, values, and entire mortal cultures would have been lost over time. Hence the need to find an alternative medium free of mortal limitations.

This new way was the phonetic alphabet, which was a unique technology. Throughout history, there were numerous kinds of writing, pictographic and syllabic, but only one phonetic alphabet used letters without semantic meaning, that corresponded to sounds, which were also devoid of any semantic meaning. With it, our words became separated from reality because they were abstractions, while reality was something concrete, that could also be presented in imagery.

> Only the phonetic alphabet makes such a sharp division in experience, giving to its user an eye for an ear, and freeing him from the tribal trance of resonating word magic and the web of kinship.[225]

Unlike speech, that oriented intersubjective communication, requiring another person to manifest ourselves, the phonetic alphabet (that implied writing), eliminated any need for "others" to communicate, replacing others with words to be "read." Reality was thus transformed from a colorful, unique, and concrete setting into black and white abstract verbal representations. In his work, Marshall McLuhan also indicated that links between individuals disappeared with the phonetic alphabet because direct communication was lost and replaced by impersonal objective claims. Again, the phonetic alphabet made information accessible without communion. This also presented additional limitations due to the fact that this medium favored individualism, and thus, societies may have suffered losses. Any media derived from language may have similar characteristics because, technologically, they arise as tools for the humans; yet another language.

Finally, in this study, we saw the function of the medium as formal cause, as suggested by Marshall McLuhan, who led us to determine that on the one hand, the medium was formal cause as it contained the information and determined a thing to be a certain way. Meaning, a medium is form, the essence of the information; however, on the other hand, a medium is a channel, connecting

---

225 McLuhan Marshall. *Understanding Media: the Extensions of Man*. MIT Press, London 1994, p. 61

two elements: the human being and reality. This "leads" individuals to behave in different ways. Also, this implies that a medium is human behavior's efficient cause, not its formal cause. A formal cause would lead a being to be, in essence, something different from what it was, and as we have seen, in reality, humans under the influence of media do not cease to be humans. Quite the contrary, we continue to be humans, but our actions are modified external devices, which are the tools we use to traverse mediated landscapes. In addition, formal cause had to do with something intrinsic to humans, and the ways that humans "used" tools were not intrinsic, but rather extrinsic. Thus, we may conclude that, in a sense, the medium is formal cause, as it determined its content. In a different sense, it was change's efficient cause, since it conditioned human behavior.

Bibliography

Anton, Corey, et al. *Taking up McLuhan's Cause: Perspectives on Media and Formal Causality*. Intellect, 2017.

Aquinas, Thomas. *Commentary on Aristotle's Physics*. Web. https://isidore.co/aquinas/Physics.htm

Aristotle. *Physics (The Complete Works of Aristotle)*. The Revised Oxford Translation, Jonathan Barnes. Ed. Princeton/Bollinger 1984).

Aristotle. *Metaphysics (The Complete Works of Aristotle)*. The Revised Oxford Translation, Jonathan Barnes, Ed. Princeton/Bollinger 1984).

Aristóteles. *Metafísica* (traducción y comentarios de Valentín García Yebra). Gredos, Madrid 1998

Aristotle. *On Generation and Corruption (The Complete Works of Aristotle)*. The Revised Oxford Translation, Jonathan Barnes, Ed. Princeton/Bollinger 1984).

Barnes, Jonathan. *Aristotle: A very short Introduction*. New York: Oxford University Press, 2000

Bostock David. *Metaphysics books Z and H*. (Translated with a commentary by David Bostock). Clarendon Press-Oxford, New York 1995

Carpenter E. and McLuhan M. eds., *Explorations in Communication: An Anthology* (Boston: Beacon Press, 1960.) http://www.questia.com/read/91604761.

Chomsky William. *Hebrew: The Eternal Language*. Varda Books, Illinois 2001

Frisch, Max. *Homo Faber: A Report* (M. Bullock, trans.). Harcourt, Inc., San Diego 1959

Gombrich Ernst H. *Art and Illusion: A Study in the Psychology of Pictorial Representation*. Princeton University Press, N.Y. 1960

Gozzi Ray. *The power of metaphor in the age of electronic media*. Hampton Press, New Jersey 1999

Havelock, Eric. *Preface to Plato*. Harvard University Press, USA 1963

Hall, T. Edward. *The Silent Language*. Anchor Books, New York 1959

Hernández, Juan Abelardo. *La Racionalidad en Marshall McLuhan y la Escuela de Toronto*. Tesis doctoral, Universidad Panamericana, 2004 (In Spanish)

Hochmuth-Nichols, Marie. "I. A. Richards and the New Rethoric". *Quarterly Journal of Speech*, 44

Humbold, Von, Wilhelm. *On Language: On the Diversity of Human Language Construction and its Influence on the Mental Development of the Human Species.* Cambridge University Press, New York 1999

Inciarte, Fernando. *Tiempo, Sustancia, Lenguaje: Ensayos de Metafísica.* EUNSA, Madrid 2004 (In Spanish)

Innis, Harold. *Empire and Communications.* Press Pocépic, Toronto, 1950

Innis, Harold. *The Bias of Communication.* Toronto Press, Canada 1951

Jung, Carl. *The Archetypes and the collective unconscious.* Princeton University Press, New Jersey 1968

Korzybski, Alfred. *Science and Sanity*, New York: Institute of General Semantics, 1993

Kroker, Arthur. *Technology and the Canadian mind,* New World Perspectives, Montreal, 1984

Macmillan, Robert. "Marshall McLuhan at the Mercy of His Commentators". *Philosophy of the Social Sciences.* 1992; 22; 475. http//pos.sagepub.com

Mahony, Patrick. "McLuhan in the Light of Classical Rethoric". *College Composition and Communication,* Vol. 20, No. 1. Feb. 1969

McLuhan, E., Zingrone, F. *Essential McLuhan.* Anansi, Toronto 1995

McLuhan, Eric. "Concerning Media Ecology." *Explorations in Media Ecology*, vol. 5, no. 3, 2006, pp. 185–198., https://doi.org/10.1386/eme.5.3.185_1.

McLuhan, Marshall. "An Ancient Quarrel in Modern America". *The Classical Journal,* Vol. 41, No. 4. Jan, 1946

McLuhan, Marshall. *Understanding Media: the Extensions of Ma.,* MIT Press, London 1994

McLuhan, Marshall. *Counter-blast.* Harcourt, New York 1969

McLuhan, Marshall. "Effects of the Mass Media". *The Clearing House,* Vol. 30, No. 9. May, 1956

McLuhan, Marshall. "Instructional Media: Is Book Dead?". *The Clearing House,* Vol. 42, No. 7. Mar. 1968

McLuhan, M. y Powers B. R. *La aldea global.* Gedisa, Barcelona 1989 (In Spanish)

McLuhan, M, McLuhan E. *Media and Formal Cause.* NeoPoiesis Press, Texas 2011

McLuhan, Marshall. "Myth and Mass Media" en *Daedalus,* Vol. 88, No. 2, Myth and Mythmaking (spring 1959),MIT Press

McLuhan, Marshall. "Teoría de la imagen". Salvat, Salvat Editores, Barcelona 1973 (In Spanish)

McLuhan, Marshall. *The classical trívium: the place of Thomas Nashe in the learning of his time.* Gingko Press, CA 2006

McLuhan, M. and Fiore Q. *The Medium is the Massage: An Inventory of effect.* Ginko

Press, California 1967

McLuhan, Marshall. *Verbi-Voco-Visual Explorations*. Something Else Press, Inc., New York 1967

Moorhouse, Alfred C. *Historia del alfabeto*. FCE, México 1982 (In Spanish)

Mumford, Lewis. *Art and technics*. Columbia University Press, New York, 1952

Mumford, Lewis. *The myth of the machine: 1*. Technics and human development. Hardcourt, New York, 1967

Ogden, C.K. Richards, I. A. *The Meaning of Meaning*. Harcourt, Brace and World. Inc. New York, 1927

Plato, *Cratylus* Web. www.perseus.tufts.edu, Plato in Twelve Volumes, Vol. 12 translated by Harold N. Fowler. Cambridge, MA, Harvard University Press; London, William Heinemann Ltd. 1921

Plato. *Phaedrus* Web. http://classics.mit.edu/Plato/phaedrus.html

Plato. *Republic,* Web. https://iep.utm.edu/republic/

Powers, Bruce. "Final thoughts: A collaborator on Marshall's methods and meanings". *Journal of Communications 31*, 1981

Richards, I. A. *Selected Essays* (1929-1974). Oxford University Press, New York 1991

Saint Augustine of Hippo. *Confessions*. Harmondsworth Middlesex. England: Penguin Books 1961

Sayre, Kenneth M. *Plato's Literary Garden: How to Read a Platonic Dialogue*. University of Natre Dame Press, 1995

Soules, Marshall. "The Bias of Communications & Monopolies of Power". http://www.media-studies.ca/articles/innis.htm, 3/Julio/2013

Strate, Lance. "If it's Neutral, It's Not Technology". *Educational Technology*/January-February 2012

Strate, Lance. "Korzybski, Luhmann, and McLuhan" en *Proceedings of the Media Ecology Association*, Vol. 11, 2010

Strate, Lance. "McLuhan", *Communication Research Trends*. 2004. Questia. Web. 30 June 2013.

Strate, Lance. *Media Ecology: An Approach to Understanding the Human Condition*. P. Lang, 2017.

Strate, Lance. *On the Binding Biases of Time: And Other Essays on General Semantics and Media Ecology*. New Non-Aristotelian Library Institute of General Semantics, 2011.

Strate, Lance. "Studying Media As Media: McLuhan and the Media Ecology Approach". *Media Tropes eJournal*, Vol. 1 (2008)

Strate, Lance, "The Deprivations of Privacy", Hannah Arendt Center, https://hac.bard.edu/amor-mundi/the-deprivations-of-privacy-2012-12-03, 3/Julio/2013

Strate, Lance. "The Fall of Nations: The Fate of Social Systems in the New Media Environment", *Revista da Associacao Nacional dos Programas de Pós-Graduacao em Comunicacao, Brasilia*, v. 14, n. 3, set./dez. 2011

Strate, L., Wachtel E. *The Legacy of McLuhan*. Hampton Press, Inc. New Jersey, 2005

Strate, Lance. "The Medium is the Memory". Library and Archives Canada. http://www.razonypalabra.org.mx/N/N80/V80/00A_Strate_V80.pdf 3/Julio/2013

Strate, Lance. "We Create the Conditions that Condition Us". Hannah Arendt Center, https://hac.bard.edu/amor-mundi/we-create-the-conditions-that-condition-us-2012-05-28, 3/Julio/2013

The Iliad, Book I. Translated by Samuel Butler. Web. http://classics.mit.edu/Homer/iliad.html

Zubiri, X. *Inteligencia y logos*. Ed. Alianza, Madrid 1982 (In Spanish)

About the Author

Laura Trujillo Liñán has a BA in Philosophy from the Universidad Panamericana, a MA in Philosophy Metaphysics from the National University (UNAM) and a PhD in History of Thought from the Universidad Panamericana in Mexico. She has been a member of the Board of Trustees of the Institute of General Semantics since 2022, as well as a member of the Media Ecology Association, the National System of Researchers (SNI) in Mexico, and the Mexican Philosophical Association (AFM). Her research topics revolve around the study of media from a philosophical perspective. She is the author of several articles and book chapters, has been an international speaker since 2011, and is currently a professor/researcher on Media and Humanities and Director of the Online University of the Universidad Panamericana.

www.ingramcontent.com/pod-product-compliance
Lightning Source LLC
Chambersburg PA
CBHW051654040426
42446CB00009B/1133